THE DESCRIPTIVE ANALYSIS OF POWER

THE DESCRIPTIVE
ANALYSIS OF POWER

JACK H. NAGEL

NEW HAVEN AND LONDON, YALE UNIVERSITY PRESS, 1975

To My Parents
Ethel and William Nagel

CONTENTS

PREFACE

> *But whoever attempts to answer these questions or define such concepts will find it laborious, and will come out, I think, with abstract...colorless propositions; rather unaesthetic and difficult, requiring hard study. Should we be afraid of that?*
>
> Chester I. Barnard

The title of this work emphasizes its limits. I use "descriptive analysis of power" to denote concepts and methods social scientists need to portray empirical systems of power. Essential elements in this analysis are a definition of power, measures of power, and principles of power inference. These prerequisites equip us to deal with other perplexing topics: indirect influence, rule through anticipated reactions, reciprocal power relations, ties between power and conflict, expansion and contraction of the total power in a system.

Except for fragmentary data in chapter 8, I offer no evidence about the distribution of power in any real society. Nor do I develop explanatory power analysis—theories, general or specific, that account for observed power structures, predict changes in them, or prescribe strategies for their overthrow.

The questions I omit have greater direct import than those with which I deal. Logical precedence dictates my conceptual and methodological preoccupation. Systematic descriptions of power systems are impossible unless we know what we mean by power, how to measure it, and how to justify power attributions. The same elements are required to develop and test explanatory or predictive power theories.

Students of power have given priority to conceptual analysis for some time. The result has been a literature that many regard, often rightly, as tiresome and sterile. I regret having to add to that literature and hope my effort will enable others to pursue more socially consequential studies.

To carry out my task, I found it necessary to resort to statistical methods, particularly Sewall Wright's path analysis. To the mathematically sophisticated, my use of statistical ideas may seem obvious, naïve, or unrigorous, for I am no mathematician. On the other hand, many readers interested in power may fear the frequent use of symbols and despair of comprehension. I hope that this will not happen, because, except for two or three passages, the text requires only patience and knowledge of algebra and basic statistics. More advanced statistical ideas are explained in chapter 5.

An earlier version of this book served as my doctoral dissertation at Yale University. I am particularly indebted to the members of my supervisory committee there. Martin Shubik, its chairman, supported the work though it turned in a direction different from the one he may have anticipated, and his close readings of drafts and detailed comments resulted in numerous improvements. Robert Dahl first stimulated and encouraged my interest in power, and his own writings on the subject were a major starting point for my thinking. To Gerrit Wolf I am grateful for constant accessibility and willingness to spend hours offering useful suggestions and trying with me to solve unsettled problems.

During early stages of my work on power, I benefited from conversations or correspondence with Karl Deutsch, J. Richard Hackman, Andrew McFarland, and Donald Stokes. Hayward Alker and Vincent McHale made brief but opportune suggestions that ultimately had a major effect on the direction of my thinking. Many persons have read drafts and helped me with comments and suggestions. At the risk of slighting others, I should mention Michael Allingham, Robert Backoff, Paul Butkovich, Corty Camann, Donald Fujihira, Robert Inman, Bernard Mennis, William Panning, Dennis Paranzino, Alvin Rubinstein, and Carlos Michelsen Terry. William Riker's thorough critique had an especially strong impact on the final manuscript. Marian Neal Ash of the Yale University

Press advised me with patience and good sense, and Nancy Paxton's careful editing resulted in numerous improvements.

As will be obvious from my citations, I have depended a great deal on writers with whom I have not conversed or corresponded, but one among them deserves special mention. In many ways, the entire thesis can be regarded as an extension and modification of Herbert A. Simon's pioneering work on power and causation. I have no reason to know whether he would agree with my analysis, but the debt should be recorded.

Financial support at certain stages of my work was provided by the Department of Administrative Sciences at Yale and by the Fels Center of Government at the University of Pennsylvania. The cost of typing an earlier version was generously defrayed by C. T. and Woo Ju Shen, and the Fels Center supported the typing of the final revision. The typing itself, a demanding task, was skillfully performed by Diane Weinstock, Lily Locke, Helene Matkevich, Mary McCutcheon, Elda Quinn, and Yvonne Smith. Diane Weinstock painstakingly constructed the arrow diagrams.

Way has always abhorred authors' acknowledgments of wifely assistance, except for Arthur Stinchcombe's comment that he "would not have married the Griselda that most authors evidently marry." In fairness, I must thank her for a great deal of help—clarifying ideas, typing parts of drafts, and greatly improving the exposition. On the other hand, if we had not decided to share marriage and the raising of two children, I might have finished this work years ago. But one does not live just to write scholarly treatises.

PART I: FOUNDATIONS

1 INTRODUCTION

In the entire lexicon of social concepts none is more troublesome than the concept of power. We may say about it in general only what St. Augustine said about time, that we all know perfectly well what it is—until someone asks us.

Robert Bierstedt (1950)

Power has long played a prominent role in discourse about human behavior. Aristotle classified political systems according to their internal distribution of power. Machiavelli instructed his prince in how to seize and secure power. Hobbes considered desire for power the wellspring of human behavior. Madison and his colleagues at the Philadelphia convention sought to design a constitutional system that would limit and disperse power. Marx, less impressed by formal devices, argued that political power inevitably accrues to the economically dominant class.

Popular thought finds the concept no less indispensable. Sloganeers depend on it: "Black Power," "Power to the People," "Sisterhood is Powerful." Political pundits cannot get through a column without it.

Modern behavioral science has embraced "power" with equal enthusiasm. "Political science, as an empirical discipline, is the study of the shaping and sharing of power," says one famous work; the same premise has been expressed repeatedly by political scientists of varied persuasions.[1] Sociologists, after a period of relative neglect, now build treatises around the concept.[2] Organization theorists struggled to explain their findings until they adopted power as a key variable.[3] "We

---

1. The quotation is from Lasswell and Kaplan (1950:xiv). See also Latham (1952), Morgenthau (1958).
2. Among the more prominent are Parsons (1963a, 1963b), Blau (1964), Etzioni (1968), and Gamson (1968).
3. Kahn (1964).

3

have been soft on power," confessed a leading psychologist, who atoned by putting together a book on the subject.[4]

Despite, or perhaps because of its ubiquity, the term power often fosters more disagreement than understanding. With the exception of Hobbes,[5] classical writers gave little attention to explicating the concept. In popular speech and writing, it is applied on the basis of intuition, preconception, or dogma. Dictionary definitions prove totally circular.

In recent decades, however, behavioral scientists have devoted literally scores of articles to defining and clarifying the concept of power.[6] It is understandable that attention should be lavished on an idea widely considered fundamental. Less understandable is the failure of this effort to result in consensus.

After surveying five leading mathematical formulations of power, Riker (1964:343) concluded:

> Even when stated verbally, these definitions have very little in common. One could not, for example, directly infer any one of them from any other.... With five definitions there are at least four distinct meanings, each of which appears quite reasonable by itself. An easy response ... is to hope that there will soon be discovered a yet more general formulation which combines these four aspects neatly into one. And yet this hardly seems possible for in some very important ways these definitions are in part mutually exclusive.

Riker felt tempted to banish the concept altogether, though he expected little sympathy from other political scientists. He misjudged the mood of at least some colleagues. March, who

4. Cartwright (1959).
5. *Leviathan*, chapter 10.
6. Twenty-seven of the best known are collected in a volume edited by Bell, Edwards, and Wagner (1969).

had earlier written three notable articles on the definition and measurement of influence, recanted in a prize-winning paper (March, 1966). "On the whole," he wrote, "power is a disappointing concept. It gives us surprisingly little purchase in reasonable models of complex systems of social choice."

Nevertheless, work on power continues unabated. Defections by senior political scientists are balanced by new recruits among sociologists, psychologists, and younger political scientists.

Why has interest in power persisted despite lack of progress? Why has attention focused on conceptualization and measurement, rather than theory construction? Why has so little agreement been achieved? Three answers to these questions will also serve to suggest some premises of this book.

Ideology

In the ostensibly scientific study of power, ideologies are challenged. Democracy ideally prescribes that everyone have equal power.[7] To judge that a few people dominate a system condemns it in the eyes of democrats. Findings of dispersed power bolster the doctrine of pluralism, a key ideological defense of the American polity. For the discontented, images of the "power structure" locate enemies and shape strategies or justify passivity.

Such ideological vested interests hinder theoretical agreement. Differing definitions of power can lead to different conclusions about empirical power distributions. As a result, scholars often fight political struggles on the conceptual battleground.[8]

Interest in the ideological implications of power research helped inspire this book. Many of its conclusions synthesize clashing ideas first propounded in partisan controversy.

7. Sartori (1962:90ff.) calls this the premise of "isocracy."
8. Social scientists are often less than candid about the ideological motivations and implications of power studies. One exception is Dahl (1960, 1969). Activists are acutely conscious of the seemingly academic dispute. For example, see Gitlin (1965).

Nevertheless, the purpose of this treatise is scientific and methodological. I strive to minimize the effect of my political preconceptions and offer no conclusions about power in existing societies.

Theory First?

A recently popular position traces stagnation in the literature about power to preoccupation with conceptual refinement at the expense of theory construction. An isolated concept can be defined and disputed arbitrarily, but a concept functioning within an empirical model stands or falls with that model, in accordance with canons of theory testing. March and other proponents of this view tend to pessimism about the usefulness of power because they assume that it should serve as "a major explanatory concept."[9] As March has shown, however, attempts to explain events adequately using the concept of power quickly lead to theories of formidable complexity.

The definition and measures I develop do entail a theoretical structure. Indeed, a virtue of the analysis will be to make explicit the theory implicit in any power attribution. But the theory needed to describe a power distribution is simple and flexible. Contrary to March, power concerns us not just as an explanatory concept, but also as an intrinsically important value. Therefore, if we can answer descriptive questions about power, the effort is worthwhile, though explanatory theory seems temporarily beyond our grasp.

Levels of Analysis

Because ideology inspires so much interest in power, attention focuses on large systems—organizations, cities, or nations. Unfortunately, most formal measures of power pertain to two-person or small-group situations. As far as I know, there exists no theoretically derived measure applicable

9. The phase is from March (1966:39). Strictly speaking, says Brodbeck (1962:286–87), there are no explanatory concepts, only explanatory statements. For other "theory-first" arguments, see Wagner (1969) and Bell (1969).

to large, *n*-person, operating social systems.[10] The various dyadic concepts seem to have differing implications for large systems, but just what the differences will be, no one can say, for such concepts cannot be transferred straightforwardly.[11] This lacuna fosters polemics and prevents resolution of disagreements. It also helps explain March's (1966) belief that power can be a useful variable in laboratory experiments, but not in nonexperimental contexts.

In contrast, the power concepts and measures I advocate derive from methods developed for multivariate, nonexperimental research. Consequently, they should be useful where earlier ideas fail to apply. At the same time, they encompass dyadic and interpersonal situations as special cases.

APPROACHES TO POWER ANALYSIS

Excellent surveys of the power literature already exist; to undertake another here would be tedious.[12] For the moment, it will be helpful only to sketch five common approaches to the conceptualization of power. Two are primitive; two achieve a higher level, but prove insufficient. The fifth will be adopted in this study for reasons to be explained shortly.

Dead Ends

The least useful way to define "power" is to substitute for it other words (e.g., "influence" or "control") that ultimately

10. One apparent exception, the power index of Shapley and Shubik (1954), measures only formal voting power.
11. A good example is provided by the work of Dahl, who developed a sophisticated dyadic measure of power (Dahl, 1957), but was unable to use it in his empirical power study of New Haven (Dahl, 1961).
12. The best historical and philosophical survey is Dahl's article in the *International Encyclopedia of the Social Sciences* (1968). Van Doorn (1963) gives a controversy-oriented introduction to the pre-1960 literature. Cartwright (1965) reviews more recent literature from several disciplines. Riker (1965) explores five mathematical efforts. Schopler (1965) and Collins and Raven (1969) emphasize studies by social psychologists. Bell et al. (1969), along with their collection of twenty-seven articles, also provide an extensive bibliography. Numerous other reviews, surveys, and bibliographies could be cited.

present virtually identical problems of operationalization and measurement. This device is employed by authors of textbooks and other works in which "power" is really to be used as it is intuitively understood—or misunderstood.

A second approach is favored by wordy savants who fill great tomes with sentences beginning "Power is...". The predicates of these sentences, usually of uncertain scientific status, include definitions, empirical propositions, speculative aphorisms, and dogmatic assertions—all mingled together in untestable form.

A third class of authors, overlapping with the group just described, devotes much attention to distinguishing types of power. Often, each type is associated with a different word from an overworked set of "power terms"—influence, control, persuasion, authority, force, violence, and so on. Some articles in this mode suggest valuable insights and distinctions.[13] Unfortunately, authors seldom agree about which label should be pasted on which idea. One writer's "power" turns out to be another's "authority," and vice versa. Furthermore, the number of distinguishable ideas far outstrips the number of available terms; a handful of words carry too great a burden.[14] Finally, little light is shed on whatever it is these different power concepts have in common.

Accordingly, like several precursors, I shall use "power" in the generic sense, encompassing the core meaning of various power terms and ignoring distinctions others make among them.

The fourth approach, though often followed, has never been better expressed than by Hobbes (1651), who described power as a person's "present means to obtain some future good." From this basic definition, Hobbes went on to identify power with such attributes or possessions as physical strength, personal skills, wealth, and instruments of war. Modern writers call advantages like these power bases, resources, or

13. Goldhamer and Shils (1939), Bierstedt (1950), and Bachrach and Baratz (1963) are among them.
14. Both points are made by Dahl (1970: ch. 3).

assets. If they are equated with power, propositions such as "the wealthy are the powerful" become tautologies (Simon, 1957). The Hobbesian version of power has, however, recently been resurrected in more abstract form by theorists who identify power with ability to reward or punish others. In chapter 11, I argue that this modern variation also renders definitional ideas that should be cast as empirical hypotheses.

Power as Causation

The fifth, and recently most prevalent, approach treats power as a type of causation. In relatively unelaborated form, the idea is not new.[15] Its current dominance is due to Simon (1953), March (1955, 1957), and Dahl (1957, 1965, 1968).[16] Their causal conception of power has attracted adherents for at least three reasons.

First, compelling similarities exist between power and cause: Both denote relations that are, in some sense, asymmetric (Simon, 1953; March, 1955). The word "influence" can be a near synonym for both "power" and "cause." When intuitive ideas of power are spelled out, they seem to be causal (Dahl, 1965).[17]

Second, causal conceptions of power avoid the danger of tautology inherent in value position or resource versions of the concept (Simon, 1953). Unless the military can use their weapons to *cause* political outcomes they favor, it seems wrong to attribute political power to them. The causal approach recognizes that the relation between guns (or any

15. Hobbes perhaps originated it. In *De Corpore* he wrote, "The power of the agent and the efficient cause are the same thing. But they are considered with this difference, that cause is so called in respect of the effect already produced, and power in respect of the same effect to be produced hereafter; so that cause respects the past, power the future time" (quoted in Champlin, 1971: 69). The fact that Hobbes can be cited in behalf of both resource and causal versions of power demonstrates their basic compatibility, a theme to which I return in chapter 11.

16. Others who stress the causal nature of power include Easton (1953), Riker (1965), Cartwright (1965), and McFarland (1969).

17. Dahl (1957) originally avoided causal terminology, but later recanted, admitting that his concept of power is causal (Dahl, 1965).

other resource) and power must be stated in an empirical hypothesis.[18]

Third, treatment of power as causation enables power researchers to employ methods developed for more general applications. Among them are experimental designs, statistical measures, causal inference procedures, and canons of theory construction. Most of this book, beginning with chapter 4, will explore benefits of transferring such techniques to power theory and research.

Two common objections to the causal approach rest on misunderstandings. To some people, causality itself is suspect. Did not Hume destroy it two centuries ago? But working scientists seem unable to do without the idea. Admitted or not, it underlies experimental design and statistical inference. Recognizing this, Simon and others have reconstructed a plausible logic of causality, free of metaphysics and compatible with Hume's strictures.[19] Chapter 4 presents Simon's model of causality in detail.

A second objection holds that causal theorists equate power with its exercise, ignoring the traditional identification of power with potentiality or capability.[20] In fact, a causal conception is compatible with any temporal point of view. Try a conjugation: "He can cause" (potential power); "she will cause" (probable or predicted power); "they did cause" (exercised power).[21] Causal theorists do concentrate on exercised power in translating their concepts into empirical operations. This is to be expected, for, as I show in chapter 11, attribution of exercised power depends upon simpler theory than attribution of potential or probable power. Power theory

18. A debate in the New York *Times* over the efficacy of nonviolence took the silly form of a dispute over the definition of power because of failure to appreciate this idea. See the letter by Chester Bowles and the reply from Eleanor Acheson, October 14 and 23, 1969.
19. Simon (1957), Simon and Rescher (1966), Blalock (1964).
20. Van Doorn (1963), Etzioni (1968), Lehman (1969).
21. Van Doorn, Etzioni, and others who define power as a capability do so in essentially causal terms, though they avoid the word "cause."

is still too rudimentary to permit rigorous empirical work on these more complex topics.

Despite these misunderstandings, the causal version of power has achieved widespread acceptance. Nevertheless, progress has been disappointing to many observers. Is the causal conception merely a useless verbal incantation, or at best an unprofitable analogy? I think not. Instead, two specific obstacles block further development.

First, theorists have not yet identified *which proper subset of causal relations should be identified with the power relation.*[22] The question has not been neglected; but, as I show in chapter 2, the answer usually offered is unproductive. In chapter 3, I suggest a better specification.

Second, much of the interest in power has centered about the search for a power *measure.* But the causal perspective offered little assistance, since no general measures of causal effect were in use among social scientists. Recently, appealing causal measures have become available. They will be described in chapter 5. In Part II, results developed in chapters 2 through 5 are combined and applied to power measurement, research, and theory.

---

22. Here I follow the traditional method of definition *per genus et differentiam* (Suppes, 1957: ch. 8). Power relations have been placed within the *genus* "causal relation," but a suitable *differentia* is missing.

2 DISTINGUISHING POWER FROM OTHER CAUSAL RELATIONS

Unless it is clearly understood that behavior may conform, because of a variety of signs indicating the preference of him who holds the power, and not merely because of commands, the phenomenon of influence remains obscure.

Carl Friedrich (1963: 162–63)

Power relations can be delimited from the broader class of causal relations by specifying the class of *effects* involved in power, or the class of *causes*, or *both*. Difficulties arise from decisions made about both effects and causes, but more serious problems stem from the class of causes commonly employed. Let us dispose first of the more tractable question.

THE CLASS OF EFFECTS CAUSED

Most modern theorists treat social power as a relation between human beings in which the effect must be *behavior* of the person controlled.[1] Objections to this position derive from two perspectives.

Psychologically inclined writers point out that insistence on behavioral effects can lead one to neglect influence over beliefs, attitudes, opinions, expectations, and emotions.[2] These hidden dispositions are of interest in their own right, and they can ultimately determine behavior. One way to admit power over such variables is to construe "behavior" to include dispositions as well as overt acts.[3] Less damaging to the language

1. Goldhamer and Shils (1930), Simon (1957), Dahl (1957, 1970), and McFarland (1969) espouse this view.
2. The argument is made by Cartwright (1959), Bachrach and Baratz (1962), and Nagel (1968).
3. Collins and Guetzkow (1964) do this.

and less misleading is the alternative of eclectically allowing any variable mentioned to be the effect.[4]

A second criticism comes from writers oriented to the study of collectivities. Whisler (1964), Lehman (1969), and Wagner (1969) argue that conventional notions focus excessively on interpersonal power and neglect control over systems. Whisler urges "removing the assumption that an individual's influence on group welfare must always be mediated by his influencing (controlling) another individual." For example, an economic elite might maintain control over national tax rates by influencing, at one time or another, a variety of individuals—presidents, key congressmen, judges, bureaucrats, lawyers, economists. For many purposes, the systemic outcome (tax structure) would be a better dependent variable than the behavior of any transient intermediary. As Lehman says, "Any *non-reductionist* analysis of power must consider the capacity to set, pursue, and implement goals for the system as a whole" irrespective of particular members.

Theorists' neglect of systemic power does not *logically* result from definitions in which behavior is the effect variable. Systems exhibit "behavior"; but social scientists who prefer behaviorist language do tend to focus on individuals.

Preoccupation with interpersonal power results also from misconstruing the relational nature of power. If power is a type of causation, then power is relational only in the sense that causation is relational. Consequently (as later chapters show), analysts should think of power as a relation between variables, not between individuals. Of course, some human relationships have a strong power component—master and slave, foreman and worker. But in *defining* power, we need a more abstract, general model.[5]

What should one conclude from this survey? First, we should restrict the effects permitted enough to confine our

4. Collins and Raven (1969) follow this course.
5. This is especially so because explanatory power theories for interpersonal and systemic levels will probably differ. Unfortunately, most recent theorizing applies only to the interpersonal level. See chapter 11.

definition to *social* power, as opposed to power over nature.[6]
Beyond that, a broad category is required to allow power over
attitudes, beliefs, collective choices, as well as over behavior.
March (1957) uses "outcome" to designate the effect variable
in power relations. This word possesses the necessary breadth,
so I shall adopt it.

In any power attribution, the outcomes controlled must be
specified by stating *domain* and *scope*.[7] The domain is the
actor or set of actors influenced—an individual, group,
collectivity, organization, nation, or whatever. The scope is
the behavior, response, attitude, belief, or choice influenced.[8]
Anyone who employs a causal concept of power *must* specify
domain and scope. To say "*X* has power" may seem sensible,
but to say "*X* causes" or "*X* can cause" is nonsense. Causation
implies an *X* and a *Y*—a cause and an effect. If power is
causation, one must state the outcome caused. Stipulating
domain and scope answers the question "Power over *what*?"[9]
Domain and scope need not be particularistic or unique.
Depending on one's purpose and the limits imposed by
reality, the outcome class may contain a few similar members
or many diverse elements.[10]

We have not advanced far toward a definition. Apparently,
power is distinguished from other causal relations more by
the type of causes involved than by the type of effects. In the
next section, I argue that existing specifications of the causal
factor are defective.

THE CAUSAL VARIABLE: INADEQUATE PROPOSALS

Theorists most frequently require that human *behavior* be
the causal variable in power relations. Many also stipulate

6. Even this distinction can be hard to maintain. See chapter 10.
7. Lasswell and Kaplan (1950) introduced these valuable concepts.
8. Inclusion of dispositions as permissible scope variables is essential to deal
with indirect power and to satisfy arguments raised by radical scholars.
See chapter 7.
9. Dahl (1957, 1970) strongly insists upon this point.
10. See chapter 8 below.

that the controller *intend* the effect he or she causes. To avoid shortcomings of such definitions, a few writers suggest that the cause be located in *perceptions* of the person controlled.

Behavior

Modern philosophy's stress on operational concepts is often misinterpreted by social scientists to dictate that their unit of analysis be observable physical acts. We have already encountered minor difficulties caused by use of "behavior" as the dependent variable in power analysis. Most writers also make behavior the independent variable in power relations. In this position it creates an impasse.

The behaviorists' methodological blinders were set in place by Lasswell and Kaplan (1950), whose work is the starting point for many modern power analysts:

> The experiential data of political science are *acts* considered as affecting or determining other acts, a relation embodied in the key concept of power.[11]

Theorists who refined and developed Lasswell and Kaplan's concepts seldom questioned their premise:

> ... For the assertion, "*A* has power over *B*," we can substitute the assertion, "*A*'s *behavior* causes *B*'s behavior." (Simon, 1957:5.)

> ... We can say that two individuals are in an influence relation if their *behaviors* are linked causally. (March, 1955: 437.)

> *A* can hardly be said to have power over *a* unless *A*'s power *attempts* precede *a*'s responses. (Dahl, 1957:204.)

> The power of *O* over *P*, as we conceive it, is concerned with *O*'s ability to *perform acts* which activate forces in *P's* life space. (Cartwright, 1959:193.)

---

11. Page xiv. Emphasis added in this and subsequent quotations.

This approach expunges from the concept of power the phenomenon known as "the rule of anticipated reactions." The phrase, coined by Friedrich in 1937, denotes a simple, ubiquitous occurrence. Whenever one actor, *B*, shapes his behavior to conform to what he believes are the desires of another actor, *A*, without having received explicit messages about *A*'s wants or intentions from *A* or *A*'s agents, then *B*'s behavior is ruled by the reaction he anticipates from *A*. Usually, of course, *B* expects *A* to reward him for conforming to *A*'s wishes and / or to punish him for deviating from them.[12]

Examples of anticipated reactions abound:

A mayor refrains from requesting a tax increase for fear of alienating voters.

A Senator supports higher appropriations for the FBI, fearing that if he does not, the agency's director will leak damaging information to reporters.

A poor woman refuses to sign a petition protesting demolition of her neighbor's house by a bank, because she fears the bank will cut off her husband's credit.

In each case, the action preferred by one party—the voters, the FBI director, the bank—occurs without its having to communicate any command, request, promise, or threat.

According to common usage and intuitive understanding, rule by anticipated reaction is a type of power.[13] Indeed, it may be true that power *usually* operates through anticipation of reactions, but the behaviorist definition excludes it from the concept. Consequently, empirical power studies by behaviorists (e.g., Dahl, 1961) are vulnerable precisely to the charge of overlooking rule by anticipated reactions (Bachrach and Baratz, 1962, 1963).

12. For other accounts of anticipated reactions, see Friedrich (1963: ch. 11) and Simon (1957: 129–30).
13. See Gamson (1968: 69). Dahl (1970) calls rule by anticipated reactions "implicit influence." Oppenheim (1961) labels it "having control," as opposed to "exercising control." (His position will be discussed below.) Friedrich (1963) appropriates the already overused "influence" (as distinct from "power") as a label for rule by anticipated reactions.

Why did this critical mistake occur? The error may have resulted partly from the unthinking application of fashionable behaviorist vocabulary. Another factor may have been an implicit conception of social causation that infuses the thinking of most people—even social scientists.

According to the convincing argument of Gasking (1955), the notion of causality originated in observation of effects produced by human manipulation. As science advances, however, this "recipe" notion of causality gives way to causation as an "inference license," in which "cause" comprises the cluster of conditions from which occurrence of the effect can be deduced. The original notion, however, remains dominant in ordinary usage and everyday thinking.

Quite possibly, many behaviorists employed the primitive idea of causation in defining power.[14] Thus, it may have seemed inconceivable that one actor could exercise power over another—cause the other's behavior—without *doing* something. As Hobbes put it long ago, in reference to power: "The efficient cause of all motion and mutation consists in the motion of the agent, or agents."[15] One who does not act cannot cause—this premise, never consciously examined, dovetailed nicely with the belief that only "behavior" could constitute a scientific unit of study.[16]

The combination of behaviorism and a manipulative, matter-in-motion concept of causation interfered even when behaviorists dealt conscientiously with anticipated reactions.

14. This speculation is less plausibly applied to Simon, who developed an advanced explication of causality. The first explanation above seems more likely in his case.
15. Quoted in Champlin (1971: 72).
16. Just as manipulative causation implies matter in motion (according to Gasking), so "behavior" usually implies bodily motion. Cf. Oppenheim (1961:15): "Behavior may be defined as any bodily movement of an organism." Only March (1955) has a different concept. He defines behavior to be "any change in the state of the organism," and then develops a formal, incompletely interpreted model of the "state of the organism." Retention of behaviorist vocabulary hinders March's thinking and helps account for his failure to resolve the problem of anticipated reactions, despite his sophisticated analysis.

Specifically, it accounts for the unsatisfactory results of noteworthy attempts by March (1955) and Oppenheim (1958, 1961).[17]

Oppenheim distinguishes "exercising control" from "having control," the latter referring to influence through anticipated reactions. Although Oppenheim would thus allow attribution of (having) power to actors who do not attempt to influence others, his behaviorist conception of causation leads him to insist that "having control" does not entail a causal relationship between controller and respondent, while "exercising control" does entail causation. This conclusion unparsimoniously implies the need for two methodologies in studying power.

March maintains that "the source and not the form of the anticipation ... is decisive" in assigning influence. This principle is indisputable when fictional actors' reactions are anticipated. Parents, not Santa Claus, induce a child to be good in order to get presents. But March extends the requirement to real actors as well, where it is less convincing. If parents teach their son to obey the law in the presence of policemen, and the youth is law-abiding in those circumstances but not in others, then it would seem that policemen do influence him when they are present.

March admits that the "agent of the predicted event" (police) may have influence, but only (*a*) by actively reinforcing the inculcated belief, or (*b*) by influencing the "agent of the symbolic communication" (parents) through a "second-level influence process." (For example: the neighborhood cop apprehends Dad committing an indiscretion. Dad then passes on the lesson to his son.) Thus March requires not only that the

17. A third effort, that of Gamson (1968: 69), raises a different problem, but deserves mention, as it is close in spirit and purpose to the approach I take in the next chapter. Gamson bases his definition of influence on a factor representing "the net result of the addition of the potential partisan group to the situation ... regardless of whether the potential partisan group has taken some action." The definition would be difficult to operationalize, as few nonexperimental groups can be added to, or removed from, their situations.

agent of the predicted event be present or perceived, but also that he *do* something.

Psychological expectancy theory can clarify March's error. Any expectancy is composed of three mental factors: an eliciting stimulus (policemen), a response to perform when the stimulus appears (obeying the law), and an expected stimulus, the goal (safety from arrest).[18] An expectancy can be established either by past experience with the elicitor *or* vicariously through symbolic processes, for example, by instruction from the "agent of symbolic communication." The response can be activated by reappearance of the original elicitor, *or* (through stimulus generalization) by appearance of a similar eliciting stimulus (any uniformed authority).

To predict occurrence of the response, one must know (*a*) that the expectancy exists and (*b*) that the eliciting stimulus is perceived. According to Simon's analysis of causality, *both* factors are causes of the response.[19] Because of vicarious learning and stimulus generalization, the actual elicitor need not have been involved, directly or indirectly, in establishing the expectancy. Furthermore, and contrary to March, the elicitor can cause the response without reinforcing it.[20]

In short, March seems to confound influence as *teaching* with influence as *causation*, a broader category. Teaching requires activity (e.g., reinforcement), whereas a passive stimulus can cause a response. Many actors whose reactions are anticipated do nothing in relation to the anticipator; they merely serve as stimuli. To avoid omitting influence through anticipated reactions, social power should be related to the wider notion of influence as causation (which encompasses teaching).

18. Hilgard and Bower (1966: 221–25).
19. Simon (1957: ch. 3). See chapter 4 below.
20. Effective stimulation without reinforcement can occur repeatedly. Research on partial reinforcement shows that a response may persist through many trials with a class of stimuli despite cessation of reinforcement (Skinner, 1953: 70ff).

Intentions

Although the behaviorist power formula is too narrow in excluding anticipated reactions, in other respects, it is too broad. One would not wish to say that *A* exercises power over *B* if *B* yawns because *A* yawned a moment earlier. Yet power as causation of behavior by behavior seems to admit such absurdities.

To avoid this, many theorists restrict power to *intended* social causation: "*C*'s behavior exercises power over *R*'s behavior if and only if *C*'s behavior causes changes in *R*'s behavior *that C intends*" (McFarland, 1969:13). This proposal encounters three difficulties. First, if, like McFarland, one tacks intentions onto a behaviorist definition, then influence by anticipated reactions remains excluded. Second, "intention" and related terms[21] connote consciousness. But an actor whose reaction is anticipated may be unaware that someone else is calculating her response. Indeed, reactions are often anticipated precisely in order to let sleeping dogs lie.[22] Therefore, even if a theorist avoids the behaviorist error in defining power, so long as he depends on intention or its near synonyms, he too will be unable to incorporate anticipated reactions. Finally, intentions are hard to prove and harder to measure. Behavioral scientists should think twice before relying on a concept that arouses such contention in courts of law![23]

Nevertheless, those who require that intentionality be included in the concept of power point to an aspect of its intuitive meaning that should be recognized. Chapter 3 nominates a more tractable substitute.

21. Weber (1947:152) refers to "will," Buckley (1967:186) to "goals," and Van Doorn (1963:12) to "purposes."
22. For a good example, see Miller and Stokes (1963). Few constituents know how their congressman votes, but if he fails to anticipate their desires correctly, the constituency may mobilize against him. Thus was Brooks Hays of Arkansas punished for moderation on civil rights.
23. Intentions are not entirely unsusceptible to empirical analysis. Cyberneticians and psychologists have made progress on this task. See the papers on "purpose" collected by Buckley (1968: part V) and also Heider (1958).

Perceptions

In an earlier attempt to include anticipated reactions in the definition of power (Nagel, 1968), I tentatively suggested a phenomenological approach:[24]

> *A* has power over *B* to the extent that *B* does something he would not otherwise do because of the existence of *A* and certain desires, intentions, and abilities attributed to *A* in *B*'s [phenomenal] field at the time that *B* makes his decision.[25]

Had I been more familiar with the literature, I would have known that there exist persuasive rebuttals to defining power in terms of what goes on inside the respondent's head. The first refutation, in its less blasphemous form, may be called the Santa Claus argument, after the March example cited above. Pure phenomenology might attribute influence over a child to Santa Claus, even though Santa does not exist. Dahl (1970:31) gives another Santa Claus example:

> A congressman who has been re-elected from the same district for thirty years is approaching senility and is totally unaware of massive changes in his district. He strongly supports farm subsidies, believing that a powerful bloc of farmers in his district will vote against him if he does not favor subsidies. In fact, however, the number of farmers in his district has dwindled to insignificance over the years, and the few who are left are happy to receive no subsidies. Are we to say, then, that our congressman is subject to the implicit influence of the non-existent bloc of farmers?

Less extreme but more realistic is the possibility that a perceptual definition might assign power to a real actor

24. In a phenomenological approach, human behavior remains the basis of observation and evidence.
25. Kadushin (1968:692) also flirts with power attributions based only on the respondent's perceptions: "As long as the person...thinks that he takes another into account, then that other person must be said to have influence."

whose desires are misunderstood by the respondent. If B does X because she thinks A wants X, when in fact A wants not-X, then it is undesirable to credit A with power over B's action.[26]

Dahl (1968) offers still another objection to phenomenological power:

> Carried to the extreme, ... this [phenomenological] kind of analysis could lead to the discovery of as many different "power-structures" in a political system as there are individuals who impute different intentions to other individuals, groups, or strata in the system.

Finally, perceptual definitions omit manipulative forms of influence such as information control and conditioning, which can be imposed independently of the respondent's awareness. Similarly, subjective concepts preclude the study of power over systemic outcomes, where a conscious respondent may be hard to identify.

These objections should not exclude phenomenology from power analysis. Investigation of subjective expectancies gives theoretical insight into processes of compliance and anticipated reactions.[27] Data about participants' perceptions assist in formulating hypotheses and provide evidence when other means of observation are impractical.[28] But to *define* power in subjective terms is a step in the wrong direction.

---

26. This danger should be distinguished from the case in which B conforms to A's *true* wishes because she misperceives A's ability or willingness to sanction her for noncompliance. Exaggerated reputation and ability to foster illusions of prowess have long been recognized as sources of power.
27. Nagel (1968); Pollard and Mitchell (1972); Bonoma, Tedeschi, and Lindskold (1972).
28. Hunter (1953); Tannenbaum and Georgopolous (1957).

3 *POWER AS CAUSATION BY PREFERENCES*

A scientific definition should be, in effect, an idealized research model for answering questions concerning the concept defined.

Russell Ackoff (1953)

In the behaviorist analysis of power, the action that A is supposed to perform before B responds is assumed to indicate, whether crudely or subtly, the response by B that A would like, feel happier about, or desire. Similarly, in the case of anticipated reactions, B expects a reward from A if his behavior pleases A, or punishment if A dislikes what he does. Correspondence between controller's desires and respondent's behavior is thus implicit in both types of power. Indeed, some notion of what is desired seems inherent not only in social power but also in all control concepts. Edwards (1964: 20, emphasis added), writing about information transmission, observes that "*any* control system functions by transmitting signals which contain information about the controller's 'desires.'"

Theorists who require intentionality or purpose in defining social power try to convey the same principle. Unfortunately, as we have seen, they employ terms incompatible with the rule of anticipated reactions.

Resorting to a simpler idea can solve the problem. In psychology and economics, the study of likes, desires, wants, values, intentions, and purposes is built upon one basic concept—*preference*. Compared to those other terms, preference connotes less about an actor's mental state and translates more readily into empirical operations.

23

In this chapter, I define power as the causation of outcomes by preferences.[1] I first explore the meaning of preference to show how use of the concept solves the problem of anticipated reactions. I then demonstrate that the proposal is compatible with a causal analysis of power. Next, a more precise definition of power is presented and explicated. After reconsidering difficulties associated with anticipated reactions, I conclude the chapter by listing merits of the proposal.

PREFERENCE AS A DISPOSITIONAL CONCEPT

Preference, the basic concept in choice theory, is usually treated as an undefined term, or primitive.[2] But several writers pay enough attention to its meaning to permit two conclusions:[3] (*a*) Preferences can be inferred from behavior, specifically from choice behavior. (*b*) Preferences are not to be identified with behavior, for a preference is a *disposition* to make certain choices, not the act of choice itself.

As a dispositional concept, preference has two properties that differentiate it from behavior. First, a preference exists over an extended time period, while a behavior is an event located in a definite relatively short time interval.[4] Second, a preference, like any other disposition, manifests itself in events only when specific conditions are fulfilled.[5]

1. Preference is not entirely a new concept in power theory. Gamson's definition of power attempts to measure a group's effect on the probability that its "preferred alternative" will be passed by a decision-making body (Gamson, 1968:69). In his 1966 paper, March uses preference interchangeably with behavior and attitudes as "initial states" to be incorporated in models of power. Dahl (1958) also uses the term but not in defining power.
2. Explicitly in Henderson and Quandt (1958:7) and Farquharson (1969:6); implicitly in Arrow (1963).
3. See Irwin (1958); Davidson, Suppes, and Siegel (1957); and Luce and Raiffa (1957:50). For a different approach, see Rescher (1967).
4. Cf. Davidson, Suppes, and Siegel (1957:16): "Choices are particular responses with a date; preference and indifference are rather dispositions which characterize an organism over a span of time."
5. Cf. Kaplan (1964:52–53): "The characteristics that make up scientific categories are likely to be 'dispositional,' that is, they identify the characters that *would* be exhibited *if* certain conditions were fulfilled."

Hempel (1952:26), paraphrasing a symbolic statement of Carnap's, suggests this form for describing dispositional properties:

If an object x has characteristic P_1 (e.g., x is subjected to specified test conditions or to some specified stimulus) then the [dispositional] attribute Q is to be assigned to x if and only if x shows the characteristic (i.e., the reaction, or the mode of response) P_2.

Descriptions of this type, known as *reduction sentences* or *conditional definitions*, differ from ordinary definitions in that they define a property only under the conditions they specify. Under other conditions, a different reduction sentence may characterize the property; or it may remain undefined. Hempel gives this example: An object is magnetic if, when put in the presence of iron filings, it attracts them; but it is also magnetic if, when passed through a closed wire loop, it induces an electric current in the loop.[6]

What test conditions and modes of response conditionally define preference? Irwin (1958, 1971) offers a reduction for preference manifested in choice behavior.[7] Drastically simplified, it amounts to the following:

If an actor is in a situation where she must choose between actions A_1 and A_2, between which she is indifferent, and she knows that A_1 will increase the probability of outcome

---

Rudolf Carnap introduced the idea of disposition concepts in 1936. For later philosophical controversy over the topic, see papers by Hempel, Pap, and Carnap in Schlipp (1963). Hempel (1952) or the first seven pages of Hempel's paper in Schlipp's volume offer good introductions. Pap's paper is especially insightful.

6. Thus, every pair of reduction sentences for a single concept implies an empirical generalization: that the same object will exhibit response P_2 when in condition P_1 *and* response P_2', when in condition P_1'. See the section on power as a disposition later in this chapter.

7. Although Irwin knew that preference should be treated as a disposition, he did not do so himself. Apparently unacquainted with the technique of conditional definition, he presented his reduction as a conventional definition.

O_1, and A_2 will increase the probability of O_2, then she prefers O_1 to O_2 if and only if she performs A_1.[8]

The easiest way to apply this paradigm is to allow the actor to determine the outcome by selecting between two costless actions—such as the statements, "I prefer O_1" and "I prefer O_2." Voting by secret ballot is an attempt to approximate this ideal.[9]

Irwin's reduction applies when an actor can affect an outcome *before* it occurs. Its relation to the behaviorist power model is evident. Given the conditions specified in the reduction, an actor reveals her preference by making an influence attempt. But those conditions do not always obtain. The action that designates the actor's preferred alternative may be costly or forbidden; or she may be unaware or unsure of how the preferred outcome depends on her own action.

We can, however, readily devise a reduction that characterizes preference by behavior *after* an outcome happens:

> If an actor is in a situation where one of two outcomes (O_1 and O_2) can occur, and O_1 does occur, the actor prefers O_1 to O_2 if, under certain conditions,[10] he expresses

8. Irwin's actual explication is in the form of a $2 \times 2 \times 2$ experimental design, varying the contingency of the outcome upon both action and setting, so the observer can discount biases due to these factors. His procedure eliminates reference to an actor's knowledge and avoids the need for using "indifference," which can be described in terms of the same operations as preference. Irwin's definition is also probabilistic. Pap and Carnap believe that in practical science, all inferences from observations to dispositions will be probabilistic. I have simplified Irwin's reduction to clarify its intuitive basis and to avoid a lengthy exposition.

9. One which often fails, due to misinformation, strategic voting, etc.

10. Determining these conditions is a problem which I leave to others, except to note some obvious candidates: (*a*) The actor must perceive which outcome occurs. (*b*) Sanctions that would inhibit his reactions must be absent.

When does influence operate through anticipated reactions? This question, worth an essay in itself, has been considered only by Friedrich (1963: ch. 11) and Merelman (1968). I suggest a few a priori principles: (*a*) When conditions favoring an influence attempt prior to the response are absent, influence, if it occurs at all, is likely to be through anticipated

pleasure and happiness, or tends to like or reward other actors he believes caused or facilitated O_1. The actor prefers O_2 to O_1, if he expresses disappointment, frustration, or rage; or tends to dislike or punish others who he believes caused or facilitated O_1.

This conditional definition, like Irwin's, is compatible with a commonsense idea of preference. It shows that an actor's preference about an outcome can be operationally characterized even when he makes no attempt to influence the outcome before it occurs.[11] Furthermore, behaviors defining his preference are precisely those the anticipation of which might induce another actor to comply.

Researchers may need additional reduction sentences to detect and measure empirical preferences; but for present purposes, the two offered suffice.[12]

PREFERENCES IN THE CAUSAL ANALYSIS OF POWER

Given the reductions above, the statement "*A* prefers that *B* do *X*" implies that if certain conditions obtain *before B* responds, *A* will attempt to cause *B* to do *X*; and/or if certain other conditions are fulfilled *after B* responds, *A* will reward *B* if she has done *X* or punish her if she has not done *X*. Since *A*'s preference, if stable, exists (as a disposition) both before and after *B*'s response, causality can be attributed to it

---

reactions. (See the preceding text paragraph.) (*b*) The respondent must perceive some probability that conditions favoring a postresponse reaction by the controller will obtain (e.g., those in the preceding paragraph of this footnote). (*c*) As in power relations generally, the controller must possess resources that make it worthwhile for the respondent to comply.

11. Can an actor exhibit conflicting preferences under the two test conditions? See chapter 7.

12. The "openness" of reduction (i.e., the possibility of adding new reductions as new facts become known) is one of its chief virtues compared with conventional definition. Openness is one of several features that closely relate reduction sentences to operational definitions. For comments on empirical observation and measurement of preferences, see chapter 8.

even when conditions for its manifestation in *A*'s behavior do not occur before *B* responds. We can devise causal schema for both processes.

In the behaviorist case, *A*'s behavior is the proximate cause of *B*'s response. *A*'s preference, however, indirectly causes *B*'s response, because it can be regarded as a cause of *A*'s behavior (figure 3.1).[13]

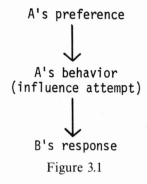

Figure 3.1

In the case of anticipated reaction, the middle step in the above sequence is omitted. We may substitute for it *B*'s anticipation (figure 3.2).

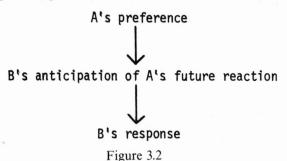

Figure 3.2

Thus *A*'s preference causes *B*'s response in both sequences, whereas *A*'s behavior is a cause in only the first. We therefore

13. Cf. Blalock (1961:18): "a relationship that is direct in one theoretical system may be indirect in another." See also Dahl (1968).

incorporate both types of power into a single definition by using preference instead of behavior as the defining cause.

Can something so immaterial as a preference constitute a cause? Die-hard behaviorists who balk at the idea of causation by a ghostly disposition should consider two arguments. First, causation is a property of theoretical systems, not of events.[14] If in useful, testable theories, disposition concepts causally precede concepts representing material events, we should not be troubled merely because our intuitive ideas of causation derive from the ricocheting of billiard balls. Second, as Kaplan (1964) and Hempel (1952) stress, disposition concepts are prevalent in all branches of science. Therefore, they often function as causes in well-established propositions.

Additional problems associated with the rule of anticipated reactions will be more easily discussed after I present the proposed power definition more formally.

A DEFINITION OF POWER

A power relation, actual or potential, is an actual or potential causal relation between the preferences of an actor regarding an outcome and the outcome itself.[15]

Actor refers, as is usual in social science jargon, to an individual, group, organization, or other collectivity. In social power relations, the *outcome* must be a variable indicating the state of another social entity—the behavior, beliefs, attitudes, or policies of a second actor.[16]

14. Here, as in other questions regarding causality, I follow Simon (1957: 50). See chapter 4 below.
15. Some readers might wish to call this relation *influence*, reserving "power" for cases in which the controller employs severe sanctions to get her way. I do not object to the distinction, but it serves no purpose at this point.
16. Recall the comments on outcomes in chapter 2, and see also chapter 8. I see no reason not to apply the definition and much of the subsequent analysis to power of human actors over nonsocial outcomes (e.g., the weather). Furthermore, autonomy, or power over oneself, might be analyzed using outcome variables representing states of the actor exercising power.

Note that the causal variable in the definition is the actor's preference, not the actor himself. The statement "*A* exercised power over *B*" is to be construed as "*A*'s preferences caused *B*'s behavior." The actor is not a variable, but his preferences are; and causality is a relation between variables in a theory, not between real objects, individuals, or events. Note also that the preference must concern the outcome caused. If *A*'s preference for X_1 over X_2 causes Y_1 to occur instead of Y_2, *A* does not necessarily have power over *Y*. Furthermore, if positive influence is attributed to an actor, his effect must be to produce outcomes ranking higher on his preference scale. When an actor's preference causes less preferred outcomes, his power is negative (Dahl, 1957).[17]

Power as a Disposition

The early part of this chapter dealt with the dispositional nature of preference. Power as I define it is also dispositional.[18] Although I presented the definition in conventional form, it can and should be interpreted as conditional: If an actor has no preference concerning an outcome, then he can have no power over it. In the absence of preference, power remains potential.

If power is dispositional, can it be defined by other reduction sentences, including one or more that apply when no preference exists? In principle, the answer must be yes, but I think it unwise at present to attempt other conditional definitions, for the following reason: As I noted above (footnote 6), every pair of reduction sentences for a single concept implies that an entity possessing the attribute in question will satisfy both reductions when their respective conditions are met.

17. The term "negative power" is more than metaphoric. Dahl's power measure and the power coefficients developed in chapters 5 and 6 (of which Dahl's is a special case) represent negative influence by negative coefficients.

18. Kadushin (1968) contends that power is dispositional, but neither develops nor adequately substantiates his belief. Instead, he uses it only as an empty "explanation" for the existence of so many different power definitions.

Given the current state of power theory, it seems unlikely that one could devise a second reduction of equal breadth that would reliably satisfy such a generalization.

Because the version I suggest is, in Ackoff's phrase, "an idealized research model," I believe greater progress will result if we use only it as a *definition*. Other conceptions of power can and should be treated as *empirical hypotheses*. Under appropriate conditions, they can be tested to see if they satisfy the definitional criterion (causality between preferences and outcomes). If confirmed, the hypothesis can take its place in power theory and, for some purposes, might serve as an alternative conditional definition or indicator of power. Chapter 11 explores these themes at greater length.

ANTICIPATED REACTIONS REVISITED

We now return to the rule of anticipated reactions, in order to lay to rest conundrums associated with the concept.

Misperception and Existence

Does the proposed definition, in admitting influence through anticipated reactions, risk attributing power to actors whose preferences others misperceive? Not at all. If B does X because he thinks A wants X, when in fact A does not, then A's preference has not caused B to do X. One will be unable to demonstrate a causal relation between A's true preference and B's behavior.[19] Referring back to figure 3.2, the causal link between B's anticipation and his behavior will remain intact, but the link from A's preference to B's anticipation will be broken, and with it, the possibility of attributing power to A, regardless of what B thinks.

The danger of misperception is essentially an objection to the phenomenological attempt to deal with anticipated reactions. Unlike the perceptual approach, the present definition and methods derived from it require observations

19. Techniques for inferring causality are presented in chapters 4, 5, and 8.

on *both B* and *A*—the behavior or other outcome associated with the former and the preferences of the latter.

This argument becomes unquestionable once it is appreciated that *B* can also misunderstand *A*'s preference when *A* overtly communicates it to him, as in the behaviorist paradigm. To take a homely example: A mother commands her son, "The grass is wet, so don't mow the lawn today;" but the boy, absorbed in a book, hears only the last four words and "obediently" mows the lawn.

One might object that the boy's responsiveness indicates the mother's "power," even though she did not get her wish in this instance. To this I would reply, agreeing with Stinchcombe (1968), that power is always restricted by the capacity of the information-carrying channels between controller and respondent. To use an old example, how great is the power of a general whose telephone lines to his troops have been severed?

The extreme version of the misperception objection to anticipated reactions—March's Santa Claus problem, in which the perceived controller does not exist—presents even less difficulty for our definition. A nonexistent entity has nonexistent preferences. Therefore, its "preferences" cannot cause any outcome.[20]

Communication and Information

Granting these rebuttals to the misperceptions argument, one may still wonder how *B* can respond to *A*'s preference if *A* does not tell *B*, directly or indirectly, what he wants. Should we not postulate with Simon (1957: 7) that the social science

---

20. Metaphorically, one might speak of the "power" of an illusion. For example, a whole society might undertake penance they all dislike heartily because they believe God wills it. It would be misleading to attribute the action to the power of the society's ruling clique, if one exists, because the rulers may like the penance as little as everyone else. The real cause is their cultural belief, and so we loosely refer to the "power" of their ideas about God. To change the society's behavior, we must alter the belief, not the power structure (unless there is some indirect tie between the two). As March (1966) emphasizes, social power does not explain everything.

analogue of "no action at a distance" is "no influence without communication"?

If we do, "communication" cannot be given its everyday meaning: the behavioral sending of words, letters, or other signals. When A's reactions are anticipated, he can remain passive while his preferences become known to B by any number of mechanisms: A may belong to a category nearly all members of which are known by B to have a particular preference. (Businessmen prefer higher profits, voters prefer lower taxes, politicians prefer to be reelected.) Sometimes the category in question comprises the entire human race. (Nearly all people prefer not to be physically assaulted.) B may infer A's preference by observing A in relations with third parties, or third parties may teach B about A. B may possess acute understanding of human motivation, or of A's motives in particular.

Thus communication can be considered a prerequisite of influence only when interpreted in its broadest possible sense. Information theory provides a good precedent. As Shannon put it, "The fundamental problem of communication is that of reproducing at one point either exactly or approximately a message selected at another point." Similarly, influence is the transferal of a pattern (or preferences) from a source (the controlling actor) to a destination (the responding actor or system), in such a way that the outcome pattern corresponds to the original preference pattern. The processes that accomplish this transmission can include, as Weaver says, "all of the procedures by which one mind may affect another. This . . . involves not only written and oral speech, but also . . . in fact all human behavior."[21]

If it means much more diverse than ordinary communication can transmit influence, how do we know when correspondence of preference and outcome indicates causation, not mere coincidence? We must resort to canons of causal inference presented in the next two chapters.

21. Quotations are from Shannon and Weaver (1949: 31, 3).

ADVANTAGES OF THE DEFINITION

To conclude this chapter, let us note six virtues of the proposed definition of power. Together they constitute a strong argument for its adoption.

1. The definition is simple, involving only two variables—preferences and outcomes.

2. It carries a minimum of substantive implications, thus avoiding the common pitfall of including in the definition of power ideas better posed as empirical hypotheses.

3. The proposal incorporates rule by anticipated reactions into a unified definition of power, without resorting to a subjective approach.

4. The definition embodies the idea that power implies ability to achieve desires, without referring to states of consciousness.

5. Its key variable, preference, has been subjected to much scientific study and is fundamental in many areas of behavioral theory.

6. Like other causal definitions, the proposal avoids identifying power with value position and points to the use of general causal methods and measures.

The utility of the definition depends entirely on the concept of causality. Its meaning can be no clearer than the meaning of causality, a topic to which our attention now turns.

4 *CAUSATION*

> *If we can define the causal relation, we can define influence, power, or authority.*
>
> Herbert Simon (1957)

In the early 1950s, having decided that power relations are a subset of causal relations, Simon undertook the necessary next step—an investigation into the meaning of causality itself. In an outstanding series of papers, he defined the causal relation for structures of mathematical equations and logical propositions. Next he established a technique for making nonexperimental causal inferences.

Simon's attempt to transfer his results to the concept of power (Simon, 1953), though important, turned out to be less thorough, rigorous, and successful than his work on causality. Part of his difficulty stemmed from the insufficient attention he gave to distinguishing power from other causal relations. An adequate definition of power did not follow automatically from his definition of causation (despite this chapter's epigraph to the contrary). The solution to that problem suggested in chapter 3 opens the way to more fruitful use of Simon's model of causality in the study of power.

This chapter begins with a relatively nontechnical summary of Simon's ideas. His concepts are then applied in conjunction with my definition of power to give an introductory demonstration of how power relations should be modeled. Finally, again following Simon, I describe and relate to power analysis some guidelines for inferring causal ordering among variables.

Why do I rely so heavily on Simon? After all, the literature on causation is immense; and Simon's approach differs from that of most authors. Three reasons justify the choice: (*a*) Simon's work convincingly translates intuitive notions of causality into scientific language. (*b*) No other analysis of causation has had so much influence among social scientists, nor has any other been so productive in suggesting practical techniques.[1] (*c*) As I intend to show, Simon's model and methods consistent with it can solve numerous difficulties in the study of power.

SIMON'S EXPLICATION OF THE CAUSAL RELATION[2]

Just as Hume, two centuries ago, insisted that "necessity is something that exists in the mind, not in objects," so Simon, employing modern terms to express the same basic idea, begins by positing that "causal orderings are simply properties of the scientist's model."[3] That is, causation is a relation between elements in a theory, not between objects or events in the real world. A conception so premised avoids objectionable metaphysical implications.

The elements of theories are variables. Depending on the analyst's purpose and the level of measurement feasible, theories can be constructed using either the two-valued variables of propositional logic or the more flexible variables of mathematics. Since one of our objectives is to measure power, I employ mathematical formulations.

1. Other discussions of causality oriented to the social sciences include Churchman and Ackoff (1950), Ackoff (1953), Timasheff (1959), Blalock (1961, 1969), Alker (1966), Buckley (1967), and papers by Dahl, E. Nagel, Samuelson, and Feuer in Lerner (1965). Essays relating power and causality include Oppenheim (1958, 1961), Riker (1965), and Dahl (1968). Many of these are compatible with Simon's thinking, although semantic differences often exist. Churchman and Ackoff, Oppenheim, and Riker all rely excessively on the distinction between necessary and sufficient causes. For a convincing argument against the use of "necessary and sufficient" terminology, see Blalock (1961 : 30–34).
2. For a more complete and rigorous treatment, consult Simon's own papers. The best starting point for those less comfortable with formal mathematics and logic is Simon (1968). Simon and Rescher (1966), though more technical, is clear and concise. The most detailed and difficult papers are chapters 1 and 3 in Simon (1957).
3. Hume (1777:224); Simon (1957:11).

When theories are expressed as equations, the initial temptation is to identify independent variables as causes and dependent variables as effects. This proposal founders on the fact that equations are symmetric. The distinction between independent and dependent variables is usually arbitrary; either can be expressed in terms of the other by inverting the function. In contrast, the causal relation is generally thought to be asymmetric, and the distinction of cause and effect is not supposed to be arbitrary.

Responding to this difficulty, Simon defines causality in terms of *structures* of equations, rather than in relation to single equations. Specifically, causal ordering requires a *self-contained structure*, a system in which there exists one equation for every variable.[4]

Not all self-contained structures can be causally ordered. For example, if every variable appears in every equation, then every variable depends simultaneously on every other variable. The requisite asymmetry is lacking.[5] The desired ordering will obtain, however, if the structure of equations can be divided into subsets in the following manner. Suppose that all the equations of a certain subset can be solved without first solving any equation not in the subset. Simon calls such a subset a minimal *self-contained subset* of the structure. More than one may exist. Together all such subsets are called the *complete subsets of zero order*. Now suppose there exists at least one additional subset such that all its equations can be solved using only the equations within it *and* the equations from one or more zero-order subsets. Any subsets of this type will be called first-order subsets. Second-, third-, and *n*th-order subsets can be defined in similar manner.

Simon defines the causal relation only for structures that can be subdivided in the way just described.[6] Specifically, the

4. This statement assumes the equations are independent.
5. Some theorists admit causality between variables which are mutually dependent. See chapter 9.
6. Systems of this type are sometimes called *block-recursive*. See Blalock (1969).

variables of complete subset C of order k are *causally dependent* on the variables of complete subset B of order j $(j < k)$ if at least one variable from B appears in C (and thus is required to solve C). In less strict language, the variables of B are said to cause, or to be causes of, the variables of C.

An`example drawn from Simon may clarify this abstract discussion. Let R represent the amount of rainfall in a given year; W, the size of the wheat crop; F, the amount of fertilizer used; and P, the price of wheat. Common sense suggests that, at least in the short run, R and F do not depend on the other variables. But rainfall and fertilizer do affect the amount of wheat grown, which in turn affects the price of wheat.

These assumed relations among the variables are most easily grasped when pictured in a diagram (figure 4.1).

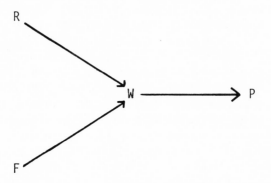

Figure 4.1

The assumptions can also be expressed as a series of equations:

$$R = R^* \qquad\qquad\qquad (4.1a)$$

$$F = F^* \qquad\qquad\qquad (4.1b)$$

$$W = f_1(R, F) \qquad\qquad\qquad (4.1c)$$

$$P = f_2(W) \qquad\qquad\qquad (4.1d)$$

Each f represents a mathematical function. The first two expressions indicate that R and F are "given"; that is, they are determined by other variables which we do not choose to investigate.

Equations 4.1a and 4.1b each constitute minimal self-contained subsets of zero order, as each can be "solved" (in a trivial sense) without employing any equation not included in the subset. Equation 4.1c is of order one, because it can be solved only by using the results of (both) zero-order equations. Finally, equation 4.1d is second order, depending as it does on the result of the first-order equation. Using the definition of causal dependence given above, one can easily see that the amounts of rainfall and fertilizer are causes of the size of the wheat crop, which in turn is a cause of the price of wheat. R and F may also be said to cause (indirectly) the price of wheat.

One additional pair of terms should be introduced at this point. If a variable appears in a complete subset C of order k, but also appears in a lower-order complete subset j, then that variable is *exogenous* with respect to C. That is, the variable is determined outside of C. In the example above, both R and F are exogenous with respect to the first-order subset composed of equation 4.1c. A variable that appears in C but not in any lower-order subset is *endogenous* with respect to C. Variable P is endogenous with respect to the subset consisting of equation 4.1d. A variable may be endogenous in one subset, but exogenous in a second higher order subset. W is endogenous in the first-order subset and exogenous in the second-order subset.

Our discussion so far has been couched entirely in terms of theoretical variables. In everyday language, however, we often speak of causation between unique events or particular objects. How are these statements interpreted in Simon's analysis? To be accepted, any such assertion must be deducible from a theoretical generalization. As Timasheff (1959) says, "Logically, statements on [the concrete] level presuppose

valid causal knowledge on the abstract level."[7] Simon (1968)
offers an example:

> A statement of the causes of World War 2 might include
> references to German economic difficulties during the
> 1930's or to the failure of the League of Nations to halt
> the Ethiopian conquest. On the other hand, a statement
> of the causes of war might include references to the outward
> displacement of aggression arising from internal frustrations,
> the absence of legitimized institutions for legal settlements
> of disputes between nations, and so on.

APPLICATION TO POWER

Using Simon's analysis of causality, it is possible to reformu-
late and substantiate the power definition presented in
chapter 3.

1. If causal relations are properties of theories, then power
relations must be also. Therefore, power and influence refer
only elliptically to social relations or structures. *Any power
attribution presupposes a theory of the outcome over which
power is presumed to be exercised.* Any empirical power study
must make its theory explicit.

2. *A theoretical structure involves power if variables denoting
preferences concerning an outcome have causal precedence over
variables denoting the outcome itself.* In other words, preference
variables must be exogenous in the subset of equations or
propositions in which outcome variables are endogenous.
More simply, within the given structure, we can know

---

7. In symbolic terms, the causal explanation of a particular event $B(a)$ requires
   both the general causal hypothesis

   $$(X): A(X) \to B(X)$$

   and the particular premise $A(a)$ (Simon, 1968).

   Given appropriate perceptual conditions, individuals may infer a
   "causal" relation after seeing only a single sequence of events. Such
   perceptions are the root of many misconceptions. The logic of causation
   in scientific methodology differs from the psychology of perceived causation.
   See Simon (1968) and Heider (1958).

preferences without knowing the outcome, but we cannot know the outcome unless we first know preferences.

The most elementary type of power theory has the following form (figure 4.2):

$$U_a = U_a^* \tag{4.2a}$$

$$Y = f(U_a) \tag{4.2b}$$

$$U_a \longrightarrow Y$$

Figure 4.2

U_a represents actor A's preference; Y, the outcome over which A exercises power. (Within equations, I use capital letters to represent variables. The letter Y indicates outcome variables, and the letter U, preference variables. Causal variables other than preferences are denoted by X. I avoid P for preference because it might be confused with power or probability.)

The common dyadic definitions of power fit this elementary model. Usually, the outcome in question (Y) is the behavior of B, over whom A has power. Existing dyadic formulations have been criticized because they do not readily generalize to situations in which more than one actor holds power. The present model easily generalizes. Consider two actors, each having some power over a single outcome (figure 4.3):

$$U_1 = U_1^* \tag{4.3a}$$

$$U_2 = U_2^* \tag{4.3b}$$

$$Y = f(U_1, U_2) \tag{4.3c}$$

Actors 1 and 2 might be congresspersons, and Y could be the allocation of flood-control funds to be divided between their districts. To predict the outcome, one must know the preference of each for flood-control funds and the function relating their preferences to the distribution of funds.[8]

8. The function can provide a measure of the power of each representative. See chapters 5 and 6.

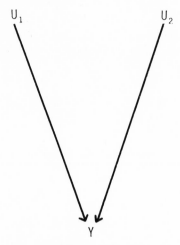

Figure 4.3

The example can be elaborated to demonstrate structures that include causal variables other than preferences. Suppose the intensity of a representative's preference depends upon the frequency of floods in his district, X_i (figure 4.4):

$$X_1 = X_1^* \tag{4.4a}$$

$$X_2 = X_2^* \tag{4.4b}$$

$$U_1 = f_1(X_1) \tag{4.4c}$$

$$U_2 = f_2(X_2) \tag{4.4d}$$

$$Y = f_3(U_1, U_2) \tag{4.4e}$$

Although flood frequencies become the ultimate explanatory variables, preferences remain the proximate cause of the outcome; and we will be unable to predict the allocation of funds without knowing $f_1, f_2,$ and f_3. Power differences will be reflected in f_3: With the same frequency of floods and the same intensity of preferences, representative 1 will probably get a larger appropriation if he is chairman of the Public Works Committee.

Still more complex structures are possible. Suppose that the entire Congress, in allocating funds, weighs not only the

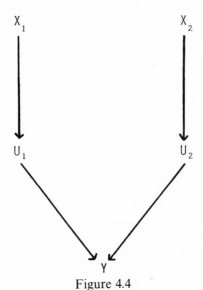

Figure 4.4

power of each claimant and the intensity of his desire, but also the merits of his claim, as indicated by the vulnerability of his district to floods (X_i). Then there will exist a direct link between each X_i and the outcome, as well as the previous indirect connection (figure 4.5).

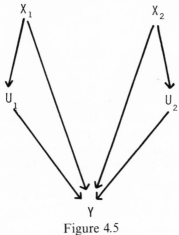

Figure 4.5

Finally, the theory can be modified to eliminate the power factor: Suppose funds are allocated according to a formula that depends only on the frequency of floods in a district. Then knowledge of representatives' preferences is not required to derive appropriations. Though they probably still exist, preferences no longer cause the outcome. If preference variables do not causally precede the outcome, then the theory is no longer a theory of power (figure 4.6).

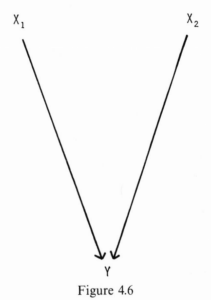

Figure 4.6

The preceding example provides only a minimal introduction to the uses and flexibility of this approach. In later chapters, more complicated structures are developed to solve key problems in power conceptualization and research. Also deferred are several bothersome questions: Can we measure preferences well enough to employ them as variables in equations? How should we decide what functions relate the variables to each other? How can we derive measures of power from the equations?

The remainder of this chapter is devoted to an even more fundamental question.

The concept of causal ordering enables one to recognize the causal relations assumed in a theoretical structure. But, in constructing and choosing among theories, how does one decide which ordering best corresponds to empirical observations?

Mathematics alone cannot provide an answer. Many different mathematical structures (in fact, an infinite number) are compatible with any solution or set of observations that satisfies a posited structure. For example, consider the pair of equations:

$$X = 6 \tag{4.5a}$$

$$Y = 2X \tag{4.5b}$$

The solution is elementary: $X = 6$, $Y = 12$. Now transform the first equation by adding the second to it. We obtain:

$$X = Y - 6 \tag{4.6a}$$

$$Y = 2X \tag{4.6b}$$

The solution remains the same; but the structure has changed. In equations 4.5, Y depends on X, but not vice versa. In equations 4.6, the asymmetry of causal ordering has been lost.

Operations like the one just performed are called elementary row transformations. Solutions are invariant under elementary row transformations, but causal orderings are not.[9] Thus, although the asymmetry of causation can be represented mathematically, there is no purely mathematical basis for

9. See Simon (1957: ch. 1) or Simon and Rescher (1966).

maintaining an assumed causal structure. Consequently, precepts and evidence from outside formal mathematics must be sought to justify any proposed causal ordering.

Such justifications fall into two broad categories: (*a*) principles for specifying causal orderings at the time theoretical equations are constructed, on the basis of relatively gross observation; and (*b*) causal inference from statistical evidence. Of the two categories, the first is more fundamental because statistical causal inference cannot be performed unless most of the possible causal sequences in a structure are specified a priori. The two classes of justification will now be treated in turn. Each discussion is followed by an account of applications in power analysis.

A Priori Causal Specification

Simon and Rescher (1966:330–34) describe four principles on which specification assumptions are often based.[10]

Temporal Sequence. Theorists universally agree that an effect cannot precede its cause.[11] This axiom often suffices to establish a causal ordering (or, more precisely, to rule out the opposite ordering) when observation confirms that one variable precedes the other. But many modern thinkers also speak of cause and effect when no clear temporal sequence exists. And, in empirical studies, time series data are often unavailable; instead, causal inferences must be drawn from simultaneous observations of variables. For both reasons, other principles of causal ordering are frequently required.

---

10. Stinchcombe (1968: 34–35) has another list of five methods for establishing causal direction. Three of his principles are similar to those of Simon and Rescher. The remaining two are implicit in the logic of statistical causal inference.

11. Teleological theories, in which a future goal functions as the ostensible cause, can be recast to preserve temporal sequence of cause and effect. See E. Nagel (1965) or Simon (1968). A more basic challenge may eventuate from the possibility, suspected by physicists, that time reversals occur in nature. So far, a search for this phenomenon by elementary particle physicists has been unsuccessful (Overseth, 1969).

Possibility of Intervention. In advanced theories, variables are related by formulas that express no causal ordering. An example is the gas law:

$$\frac{PV}{T} = k \qquad (4.7)$$

where P = pressure, V = volume, T = temperature, and k represents a constant. Despite the symmetry of this expression, asymmetry may result from intervention. If we light a fire under a balloon, we say that the higher temperature causes increased volume and pressure.[12]

Stinchcombe (1968 : 34–35) observes that one can manipulate effects as well as causes. If intervention changes Y, and X does not change, then Y does not cause X. If known covariation of X and Y has previously convinced us that some causal connection exists, we deduce that X must cause Y. An example of Gasking's illustrates the point. Changing the color of metal does not affect its temperature. Therefore, we infer that heating a metal causes color changes, rather than vice versa.

Temporal sequence and intervention, together or separately, justify causal specification in experiments. In nonexperimental situations, however, conclusions must be built upon less sure foundations.

Prepotence. Common sense suggests that it is harder for the small to affect the large than for the large to affect the small. Simon and Rescher generalize this notion by noting that we usually assume "the behavior of any system involving very large quantities of energy (e.g., the atmosphere) is practically autonomous of the behavior of variables involving very much less energy (e.g., wheat growing)." This they call the principle of prepotence.

Known Mechanism.[13] Much difficulty is avoided if, out of the practically infinite number of pairs of variables, no two

12. The example is adapted from Simon and Rescher (1966). Gasking (1955) offers other physical science examples. Feuer (1965) and Samuelson (1965) also stress the role of intervention in causation.
13. Called by Simon and Rescher the "Postulate of Independence, or, more vividly, the Empty World Postulate."

are assumed to be related without good reason. "Good reason" to the scientist means that a known mechanism exists by which one variable might influence another. For example, the size of the wheat crop can be assumed to affect the price of wheat through the mechanism of supply and demand, the validity of which we accept.[14]

Although the known mechanism principle can be helpful, its use involves an element of complacency, amounting to the tacit assertion that we already know all applicable causal laws. This can be dangerous in the social sciences, where well-substantiated laws are rare.[15]

Specification in Power Analysis

Each of the preceding principles can be, and has been, employed to justify assumptions about the direction of social influence.

Temporal Sequence. If, in succession, the president announces his opposition to a bill, opinion polls reveal overwhelming public favor for the same bill, and the president reverses his position, then it is plausible to attribute influence to the public. Conversely, since polls showed little public interest in Vietnam until President Johnson decided to attack it, whereupon the great majority voiced support for his policy, we infer the president influenced public opinion (at early stages of the war) rather than the other way around.

Temporal succession, traditionally associated with causality, has by extension been considered by many an essential property of power relations. The decision-making method of

14. The known mechanism principle can also be interpreted more loosely as encouraging respect for hypotheses that have "density" or "continuity" —i.e., those for which one can specify additional events and principles intervening between the cause and effect. (The terms "density" and "continuity" come from Samuelson, 1965.)
15. The postulate of independence also seems to run afoul of the "First Law of Ecology: everything is connected to everything else" (Commoner, 1971:29). But not everything is directly and simultaneously connected to everything else. See chapter 9 below.

studying power, developed by Dahl and his students,[16] relies almost exclusively upon this principle. The method assigns power over any positive decision to the actor who initiated it. Unfortunately, behavioral initiation does not necessarily entail power as I have defined it. New Haven's Mayor Lee initiated most redevelopment policies during his term in office, but perhaps his programs were tailored to conform to correctly anticipated preferences of the city's commercial magnates. Conversely, if favorable business response to his proposals resulted from the mayor's persuasive skill—i.e., if Lee's preferences caused the businessmen's preferences—then power can be attributed to him.

Behaviors are historical events; their temporal sequence is easy to establish (in principle, if not always in practice). In contrast, severe difficulties, both theoretical and practical, arise in establishing temporal priority among preferences, since they are covert, temporally extended dispositions.[17] As earlier examples suggest, attitude surveys can assist in providing time-series data; but even with more systematic and far-reaching surveys than we now have, the principle of temporal sequence will not always suffice to establish causal specifications needed in power research.

Intervention. Experiments are possible in the study of power; and experimenters can determine preferences through instruction, manipulation, or selection of subjects. Corresponding variations in outcomes would then permit conclusions about power in the experiment. Interest in power, however, centers about nonexperimental situations. Even here there is some possibility of intervention, though it cannot be used with the same experimental rigor. A lobbyist, for example, attempts to change preferences of those she believes have power. If she succeeds and social policy also changes, her power hypothesis is strengthened. Even social scientists, when acting as policy advocates, must test their knowledge of the power structure.

16. Dahl (1958, 1961) and Polsby (1963).
17. See chapters 7 and 8.

Nevertheless, opportunities for intervention are limited. Some preferences are immutable; others, modifiable only at prohibitive material or moral cost.

Prepotence. When a southern congressman opposes civil-rights bills, we readily infer that he is conforming to the desires of the majority in his district. Actually, the correlation of his statements and his constituents' biases could equally allow the inference that the representative influences his district. Implicitly, however, we rely on the principle of prepotence to establish the direction of causation. To do so seems reasonable: The representative is one usually rather inconspicuous individual; his constituency numbers hundreds of thousands.

Limitations of prepotence as a guide to specification become apparent, however, when one recalls the earlier examples of influence relations between president and voters. We have no difficulty in believing that the president influences the national electorate; yet he is only one against millions. In social systems, amounts of energy or mass are less important than flows of information in highly organized communications networks. Simon and Rescher's prepotence principle offers little help in studying such systems. If slavishly followed, it could even rule out all theories of dictatorship and elite rule.

Known Mechanism. Power theorists echo this precept by stipulations that some "connection" or communications link must exist between controller and respondent (Simon, 1957; Dahl, 1957). As I contend in chapter 3, "communication" must be interpreted liberally, or else the condition screens out power relations involving anticipated reactions and information manipulation. Thus, this application of the known mechanism principle does not help in determining the direction of influence as much as was once imagined.

The known mechanism principle is also reflected in our readiness to attribute power to actors who control key incentives. Because we believe that most people are motivated to protect their physical safety and economic well-being, it is easy to ascribe power to generals and capitalists. This does not take us far. Do generals have power over persons willing to die for a cause? Can capitalists control ascetics? Who dominates when generals and capitalists conflict? Behavioral scientists know too little to rely securely on known mechanisms.

The preceding discussion leads to several conclusions: Simon and Rescher's four specification principles often serve to guide tentative judgments about the direction of social influence; sometimes they permit decisions to be made with a fair degree of confidence. Obviously, power researchers should develop data and theory that permit more frequent use of the principles. Nevertheless, at present and during the foreseeable future, a priori guides to specification will often be inapplicable, or conflicting, or otherwise inadequate. Some other method is needed to decide the direction and sometimes even the existence of social influence.

Statistical Causal Inference

Fortunately, Simon (1957: ch. 2) devised such a technique. His method, as extended and elaborated by Blalock (1961), has become well known in the social sciences.

In simplest form, the Simon–Blalock technique of causal inference applies to situations in which (*a*) a correlation is observed between two variables, X_1 and X_2; and (*b*) the researcher does not know whether the correlation indicates a true causal relation and / or does not know in which direction the causal influence operates. Figure 4.7 diagrams the three possibilities. In (*c*), the correlation is spurious; it is entirely accounted for by the common cause, X_3.

Various reasons can account for the researcher's inability to select among the three alternatives. Perhaps none of the a priori guides is available; or, two or more bases of specification yield conflicting results; or, reasons for specification exist but are not fully convincing, so that further evidence is desired.

In such cases, Simon argued, causal inferences about the link in question can be made, provided three requirements are

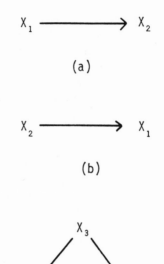

(a)

(b)

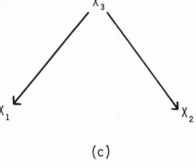

(c)

Figure 4.7

met : (a) A third variable correlated with either or both of the original variables can be observed.[18] (b) A priori principles of specification justify assumptions that some logically possible causal connections among the three variables do not exist (other than the link in question). (c) Necessary assumptions can be made about variables not in the model.

Given these requirements, the values of certain partial correlation coefficients entail causal inferences. For example, if no causal relation exists between X_1 and X_2, then the partial

18. Blalock extended the method to models with more than three variables.

correlation $r_{12 \cdot 3}$ should equal zero. When the $X_1 - X_2$ relation is nonspurious, the direction of causation between the two can be inferred from more complicated relations among partial correlations.[19]

Causal Inference in Power Analysis

Several authors have noted the relevance of the Simon–Blalock technique to power studies (Dahl, 1968; McFarland, 1969; Bell et al., 1969). Nevertheless, applications of the method in empirical power research are almost nonexistent.[20] I suspect that three reasons account for this lacuna. First, until recently, knowledge of the method and sufficient statistical skill to use it were not widespread among social scientists concerned with power.[21] Second, as I argue in chapter 2, prevailing definitions of power did not point to a readily measurable causal variable. Third, the Simon–Blalock technique permits only qualitative conclusions about the existence or the direction of causal relations. Students of power, however, often ask quantitative questions—not whether a group exercise *some* power, but whether it has *more* influence than its competitors. Therefore, researchers need not only a technique of causal inference, but also a way to measure causal influence.

In the last decade, social scientists have been introduced to a method which, encompassing the Simon–Blalock technique as a truncated special case, makes possible both causal inference and causal measurement. This procedure, path analysis, can serve as a basic tool for investigating power on either the conceptual or the empirical level.

19. I have given only a superficial account of the causal inference method because it has been superseded by path analysis.
20. Cnudde and McCrone (1966) used it to reanalyze Miller and Stokes' constituency influence data. They did not emphasize power implications of their work, but Bell et al., point out its relevance by including it in their anthology.
21. Even those who attempt the technique sometimes display deficient understanding. See the critique of Cnudde and McCrone and others by Forbes and Tufte (1968).

5 PATH ANALYSIS

> *The concept of cause is only significant when there are differ-*
> *ent degrees of causation that can be measured. To give causation*
> *degrees means to correlate changes in initial conditions with the*
> *corresponding changes in later conditions. This requires the*
> *entire apparatus of statistics and probability.*

> Arturo Rosenblueth and Norbert Wiener (1950)

If power relations are a subset of causal relations, then methods for measuring and inferring causality should apply to power. This chapter explicates path analysis, an intuitively appealing technique for causal measurement and nonexperimental causal inference. Path analysis is already practical for some empirical power studies, and its potential for such use should increase in the future. Given the present backward state of theory and data, however, its most useful immediate application may be to improve conceptual and theoretical analysis, a contention which I hope subsequent chapters will justify.

In order to shorten a necessarily complicated development, this chapter contains few references to power. Readers already acquainted with path analysis should proceed to Part II.

The methods to be presented stem from a remarkable instance of similar, but largely independent development in different disciplines. Beginning about 1920, the geneticist Sewall Wright invented path analysis as a device for causal interpretation of statistical correlations. During the 1930s and 1940s, econometricians made great strides in the use of empirical data to estimate parameters in systems of simultaneous equations. Finally, Simon and Blalock tackled the problem of testing causal hypotheses nonexperimentally. Although they drew heavily on econometrics, they were so preoccupied with causal inference that they neglected the possibility of estimating parameters in the models they wished to test.

Not until 1965 were the three streams united. Raymond Boudon, a French sociologist, developed "dependence analysis" by starting from the Simon–Blalock assumptions and then deriving parameter estimates. Boudon discovered that his dependence analysis led to the same formulas as Wright's path analysis, at that time almost unknown in the social sciences.[1] A year later, the sociologist Otis Dudley Duncan published the first introduction to Wright's work for social scientists. Duncan drew on econometric techniques in several empirical applications of path analysis. Since then, examples of cross-fertilization have become numerous.

Although this chapter emphasizes the framework and algorithms of path analysis, the exposition borrows from all three literatures. No attempt is made to be complete or rigorous. I intend only to enable the reader to understand power applications in later chapters. Anyone who plans to use the techniques discussed should study more advanced sources.[2] The econometrics literature especially should be consulted for guidance on specialized problems.

1. Miller and Stokes (1963) were probably the first social scientists to mention path analysis, but they did not employ the method.
2. Introductions to path analysis for social scientists include Duncan (1966), Heise (1969), Land (1969), Alker (1969), and Stokes (1971). Applications are reported in Blau and Duncan (1967), Borgatta and Bohrnstedt (1970), Duncan, Haller, and Portes (1968), and Duncan (1966, 1969). Other pertinent discussions are Blalock (1968b) and Tufte (1969).

   Wright developed and applied his method in papers spanning four decades. Most of his ideas are now available in his three-volume *Evolution and the Genetics of Populations* (1968). See especially volume 1, chapters 13 and 14. Other discussions by geneticists and statisticians include Li (1955), Tukey (1954), and Turner and Stevens (1959).

   Boudon presented his very similar dependence analysis in two articles in English (Boudon, 1965, 1968) and, with greater detail, in his book *L'analyse mathématique des faits sociaux* (1967). His technique for parameter estimation has been criticized by Goldberger (1970).

   The econometrics literature is difficult, and many social scientists may prefer Blalock (1969) and other interpreters. In preparing this chapter, however, I found Johnston (1963), Goldberger (1964), and Fisher (1966) helpful when less technical sources were inadequate.

   Articles from all three traditions have been made more accessible with the recent appearance of collections edited by Blalock (1971) and by Goldberger and Duncan (1973). Another useful source is the annual *Sociological Methodology*.

ELEMENTS OF CAUSAL MODELING

Any attempt to measure causation must begin with a model that incorporates hypothetical causal relations among a set of variables. Both equations and diagrams can represent causal models. Since equations are more fundamental in estimating coefficients, I begin with them.

Structural Equations

Path analysis and related techniques ordinarily require that assumed causal relations be expressed in the form of linear equations. This means that, in any equation, the total value of the effect variable is assumed to result from the sum of separate effects of each causal variable; and the effect of each causal variable depends on the value of the variable itself, not on its square, cube, or some higher power. Not all causal relations are linear. Nevertheless, the linearity assumption is worthwhile for at least three reasons: (a) Unless there is reason to assume a more complicated relation, it is convenient to stick with the simple linear form. (b) Even when the actual relation is nonlinear, a linear equation sometimes gives an acceptable approximation. (c) Many nonlinear relations can be expressed in linear form by devices discussed later in this chapter.

Assuming linearity, the equation for the *j*th variable of a set of *n* variables has the following general form:

$$X_j = a_{j1}X_1 + \ldots a_{ji}X_i + \ldots + a_{jn}X_n \qquad (5.1)$$

The coefficients a_{ji} represent the strength of the effect of X_i on X_j.[3] If the causal ordering is correct, a unit change in X_i should result in a change of a_{ji} units of X_j.

Equation 5.1 indicates that X_j is entirely determined by the other $(n - 1)$ variables in the equation. In empirical

3. The first subscript represents the dependent variable; the second, the independent variable. This is the convention in both regression and path analysis, but Boudon (1967) uses the reverse pattern.

It is assumed that all variables are measured in deviations from their means. This eliminates intercept terms, but has no effect on coefficients.

applications, however, one is seldom able to make this assumption. Factors not included in the equation may affect the observed values of X_j. Among them are (a) causes unknown to the investigator; (b) causes that cannot be measured; (c) measurement errors; (d) errors resulting from imperfect approximation to linearity; and (e) random fluctuations (unless one believes in strict determinism). All these possible effects are incorporated by adding to the equation an extra term, R_j, variously described as the residual, disturbance, or error term:[4]

$$X_j = a_{j1}X_1 + \ldots + a_{ji}X_i + \ldots + a_{jn}X_n + a_{jj}R_j \qquad (5.2)$$

As we learned in chapter 4, causal orderings are properties of structures of equations, not of isolated equations like 5.2. In particular, a self-contained structure is required—one with an equation for every variable. A self-contained structure for n variables can be represented by a system of n simultaneous equations:

$$X_1 = a_{12}X_2 + \ldots + a_{1i}X_i + \ldots + a_{1n}X_n + a_{1a}R_a$$
$$(5.3a)$$

$$\ldots\ldots\ldots$$

$$X_j = a_{j1}X_1 + \ldots + a_{ji}X_i + \ldots + a_{jn}X_n + a_{jj}R_j \qquad (5.3j)$$

$$\ldots\ldots\ldots$$

$$X_n = a_{n1}X_1 + \ldots + a_{ni}X_i + \ldots + a_{nn}R_n \qquad (5.3n)$$

Although system 5.3 is self-contained, it is not causally ordered according to Simon's definition. Furthermore, its coefficients cannot be determined empirically; they are not identifiable.[5] Both defects of the structure can be better

---

4. In diagrams and examples, I shall give the residual a letter subscript corresponding to the number subscript of the dependent variable. For example, the residual of X_1 will be R_a. This representation combines the notations of Wright and Stokes. Assignment of a coefficient to residuals is customary and useful in path analysis. In econometrics, the residual of X_1 would usually be represented by e_1 or u_1, without a coefficient.

5. Simon (1957:ch. 1) shows that causal ordering and identifiability are closely related, though not equivalent.

explained after introducing distinctions among types of structures.

Types of Equation Structures

In the general simultaneous equation system represented by 5.3, it is assumed that, for any i and j, both a_{ij} and a_{ji} are nonzero. X_i affects X_j, and X_j affects X_i; the variables are mutually determined (figure 5.1).

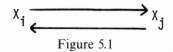

$$X_i \rightleftarrows X_j$$

Figure 5.1

Reciprocal influence can also occur indirectly, through loops (figure 5.2).

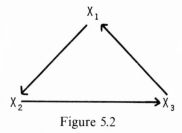

Figure 5.2

X_1 affects X_2 directly; X_2 in turn influences X_1 via X_3.

In an important class of structures known as *recursive* systems, both types of mutual determination are excluded; only one-way causation is permitted. Variables in recursive systems can be numbered in such a manner that $a_{ij} = 0$ for all $i < j$. This means that the equations can be arranged in the following triangular pattern:[6]

6. In equations 5.4 all terms except disturbances have been shifted to the left side in order to reveal more clearly the structure of the coefficient matrix.

   Fisher (1966:96) reserves the term "recursive" for structures that have *both* a triangular coefficient matrix (i.e., $a_{ij} = 0$ for all $i < j$) *and* uncorrelated disturbances. I follow the usage more common among noneconomists both to prevent confusion and to give more prominence to the restriction on disturbances.

$$X_1 \qquad\qquad\qquad\qquad = a_{1a}R_a \qquad (5.4a)$$

$$-a_{21}X_1 + X_2 \qquad\qquad\qquad = a_{2b}R_b \qquad (5.4b)$$

$$-a_{31}X_1 - a_{32}X_2 + X_3 \qquad\qquad = a_{3c}R_c \qquad (5.4c)$$

$$\cdots\cdots\cdots$$

$$-a_{n1}X_1 - a_{n2}X_2 - a_{n3}X_3 - \ldots + X_n = a_{nn}R_n \qquad (5.4n)$$

It is easy to see that recursive systems are causally ordered. In system 5.4, 5.4a is a minimal self-contained subset of zero order, 5.4a plus 5.4b constitute a self-contained first-order subset, 5.4a, 5.4b, and 5.4c are a self-contained second-order subset, and so on. In other words, X_1 causes X_2; X_1 and X_2 are causes of X_3, etc.

Pure recursive systems are a special type of causally ordered structures. The more general category, *block recursive* systems, can be divided into subsets, or "blocks," within which there may be reciprocal influence. Between blocks only one-way influence occurs.[7] Figure 5.3 is an example, adapted from Blalock (1969:72).

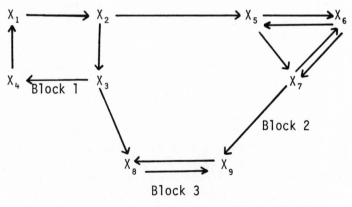

Figure 5.3

7. For an introduction to block recursive systems, see Blalock (1969). Fisher's (1966: 99–100) definition stipulates that disturbances from different blocks must be uncorrelated, in addition to requiring a block triangular coefficient matrix. (See the preceding footnote.)

The recursiveness of the system becomes apparent when a single letter represents each block (figure 5.4).

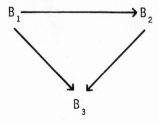

Figure 5.4

In simple recursive systems, each block is composed of just one variable.

Block recursive systems and causally ordered systems are equivalent; a structure is causally ordered if and only if it is block recursive. Each block, together with directly connected variables from lower-order blocks, constitutes a self-contained subset. In figure 5.3, block 1 is a self-contained zero-order subset; block 2 plus X_2 form a first-order self-contained subset; and block 3 plus X_3 and X_7 constitute a second-order self-contained subset. Within blocks, variables are not causally ordered. Between blocks, causal relations do exist. All variables in block 1 are direct or indirect causes of all variables in blocks 2 and 3.

Implications for the study of power are clear: If power relations are causal relations, and if Simon's definition of causality is accepted, then any power hypothesis can, in principle, be represented by a block recursive structure.[8] Furthermore, preference variables must appear in a lower-order block than do variables representing the outcome in question. At present, however, I shall not pursue applications to social influence. Instead, we are ready to use these distinctions among structures in discussing how to estimate coefficients.

8. The "in principle" should be stressed. For reasons discussed in chapter 9, it may be necessary to weaken this conclusion in practice.

Estimation and Identifiability

Unfortunately, estimation is mathematically impossible for many structures. An adequate explanation of this difficulty, the problem of *identification*, would require far more attention than can be devoted to it here.[9] Only a crude sketch will be given. Essentially, lack of identifiability results when one attempts to take from an analysis more information than has been put into it. The *desired* information consists of estimates of coefficients and residuals. The information *given* is a set of observations of the n variables. In an unrestricted model (e.g., equations 5.3), $n(n - 1)$ coefficients must be estimated, along with n residuals. In contrast, the known information is summarized in only $n(n - 1)/2$ covariances (or correlations), one for each pair of variables.

The problem can sometimes be overcome by furnishing additional information in the form of a priori assumptions. These assumptions typically concern correlations involving residuals or exclusion of coefficients.

The most common restriction on residuals is the premise that residuals of endogenous variables have zero correlations with each other and with exogenous variables.[10] Since this assumption is almost invariably made, a word about its theoretical import is in order. Any correlation between residuals may, in theory, be interpreted causally by supposing that a factor included within one residual causes a factor included within the other, or that some third factor causes elements of each. If all such causally connected elements are brought explicitly into the model, then the correlation between residuals will vanish. Thus to assume uncorrelated residuals is to presume that the theoretical structure is complete—i.e., that no factor significantly affecting two or more variables has been omitted (Heise, 1969).

9. Blalock (1969) provides a good introduction for social scientists. Fisher (1966) is a definitive source. My presentation largely follows Heise (1969).
10. The "residuals" of exogenous variables (the two are equivalent), may be correlated. See the discussion of multicollinearity later in this chapter.

The best justification for the restriction on residuals is a scrupulous effort to seek omitted variables that might invalidate the assumption. If such factors are discovered, the model should be "enlarged" or "completed" by incorporating them. Consider a correlation between the residuals of two variables (figure 5.5).

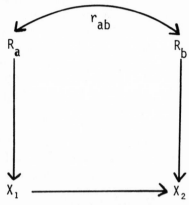

Figure 5.5

If an element W_2 in residual R_b causes an element W_1 in R_a, both should be brought into the model, hopefully eliminating the correlation between the new residuals R_a', and R_b' (figure 5.6).

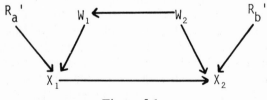

Figure 5.6

The problem, of course, is to know when residuals are correlated, and then to discover the implicit factors within them that account for the correlation.[11]

11. Tufte (1969) has suggestions and references.

Exclusion assumptions are closely related to specification of a causal ordering. If a sufficient number of coefficients in the proper (block recursive) pattern can be assumed zero a priori, then the structure is causally ordered; but not all coefficients will necessarily be identifiable. Here enters the peculiar advantage of simple recursive systems. By permitting only one coefficient for each pair of variables instead of two, recursiveness cuts the number of coefficients to be estimated in half.

Recursiveness *alone* does not guarantee identifiability.[12] If, however, the assumption of recursiveness is combined with the postulate that residuals of endogenous variables are uncorrelated with each other and with exogenous factors, then the structural coefficients are *always* identifiable.[13] Furthermore, given these two assumptions the best estimator of the coefficients will be ordinary least-squares regression, applied to each equation separately.[14]

These two properties—identifiability and applicability of ordinary least squares—make the assumptions of recursiveness and uncorrelated errors popular among practitioners of path analysis, causal inference, and related techniques. Sometimes the two premises are treated as essential for estimation, although in fact neither is necessary.[15]

In nonrecursive systems (including block recursive structures), the added estimation burden posed by reciprocal relations among some variables may be offset by postulating zero relations between other variables (Heise, 1969). But estimation techniques that are more complicated than least squares will be necessary.[16]

12. For a demonstration, see Boudon (1967: 90–92).
13. For proofs, see Fisher (1966: 118–121) or Boudon (1967: 93–96). (Note that Boudon assumes a triangular coefficient matrix without explicitly stating so.)
14. "Best" in that the estimate will be unbiased and have minimal variance (Goldberger, 1970). See also footnote 35 below.
15. For necessary and sufficient conditions of identifiability, see Fisher (1966) or, for a less technical statement, Blalock (1969: 64–66).
16. For examples of estimation in nonrecursive models, see Duncan, Haller, and Portes (1968), Wright (1960), and Alker (1969).

Consequently, power analysts who wish to employ linear estimation techniques will have an easier time with situations that can be modeled as recursive systems. But if reciprocal links cannot be ruled out, it is not always necessary to abandon hope. Conditions for identifiability must be kept in mind, however, for models that do not satisfy them are useless in empirical research.

DERIVATION OF KEY RESULTS

Path analysis does not really differ from standard linear estimation methods. Instead, it extends them to provide an appealing pattern for interpreting causal structures, and a convenient technique for calculating indirect effects (Duncan, 1966).

Path Coefficients

The theory of path analysis can be presented as beginning with estimation of coefficients for the structural equations. Wright calls these parameters *path regression coefficients*. They are merely the coefficients obtained by standard estimation techniques. A typical structural equation would then be:

$$X_j = \sum_i a_{ji}X_i + a_{jj}R_j \qquad (5.5)$$

in which the X_i are all variables that directly affect X_j.

Now standardize X_j by dividing through by its standard deviation, s_j. Following convention, we represent standardized variables by Z:

$$X_j(1/s_j) = Z_j = (1/s_j)\left[\sum_i a_{ji}X_i + a_{jj}R_j \right] \qquad (5.6)$$

Next, multiply each term on the right side of 5.6 by (s_i/s_i):

$$Z_j = (1/s_j) \sum_i a_{ji}X_i(s_i/s_i) + a_{jj}R(s_{Rj}/s_{Rj}) \qquad (5.7)$$

Assume that $s_{Rj} = 1$; and define the path coefficient, d_{ji}, as follows:[17]

$$d_{ji} = a_{ji}(s_i/s_j) \qquad (5.8)$$

Finally, write all variables in standard form, and substitute path coefficients for path regressions:

$$Z_j = \sum_i d_{ji}Z_i + d_{jj}R_j'. \qquad (R_j' = R_j/s_{Rj}) \qquad (5.9)$$

Equation 5.9 is a standardized version of 5.5. The path coefficient is merely a standardized structural coefficient (path regression), equivalent to the beta weights of multiple regression.[18]

Path Diagrams

More interesting developments in path analysis are best presented with the aid of path diagrams. Though similar to the causal diagrams in chapter 4, Wright's device includes additional information: (*a*) Arrows are drawn from each assumed cause to its immediate effects. (*b*) The appropriate path coefficient is written alongside each arrow. (*c*) Residuals and their path coefficients are depicted. (*d*) A curved, double-headed arrow connects each pair of exogenous variables, representing their correlation, which is written beside the curved arrow.[19] The following illustration is used in subsequent developments (figure 5.7).

Indirect and Total Effects

I shall first employ the model depicted by figure 5.7 to illustrate a useful result of path analysis, the calculus of

17. The symbol p_{ji} is conventionally used for path coefficients. I employ d_{ji} to avoid confusion with "probability" or "power." Boudon used d to represent his standardized dependence coefficients, which are equivalent to Wright's path coefficients.
18. On beta weights, see Blalock (1960: 343–46).
19. Residuals and / or correlation arrows are omitted when their presence would clutter the diagram. But their existence must be remembered, unless there is reason to consider them insignificant.

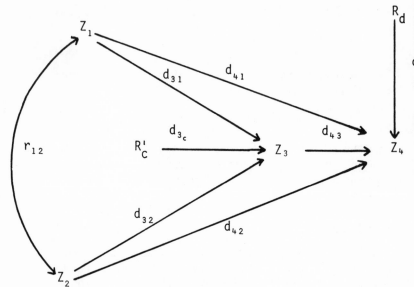

Figure 5.7

indirect and total causal effects. The path equations for the model's endogenous variables are:[20]

$$Z_3 = d_{31}Z_1 + d_{32}Z_2 + d_{3c}R_c' \qquad (5.10a)$$

$$Z_4 = d_{41}Z_1 + d_{42}Z_2 + d_{43}Z_3 + d_{4d}R_d' \qquad (5.10b)$$

Substitute equation 5.10a in 5.10b and collect terms:

$$Z_4 = (d_{41} + d_{43}d_{31})Z_1 + (d_{42} + d_{43}d_{32})Z_2$$
$$+ d_{43}d_{3c}R_c' + d_{4d}R_d' \qquad (5.11)$$

From 5.11, it can be seen that the total effect of, e.g., Z_1 on Z_4 is the sum of two terms—d_{41}, which measures the contribution of the direct link between the two variables, and $d_{43}d_{31}$, which measures the impact of the indirect link through Z_3. Along any path, the *indirect effect* is measured by the *compound path coefficient*, d_{kji}, the product of simple path coeffi-

20. Derivations in the next few paragraphs are based on Stokes (1971).

cients connecting the ultimate cause and the final effect. In the example:

$$d_{431} = d_{43}d_{31}. \tag{5.12}$$

In recursive systems, the *total effect* of any variable upon any other is given by the sum of path coefficients, simple or compound, across all paths connecting the two variables. (Paths traced along curved correlation arrows do not count in calculating a variable's total effect because they have no causal interpretation.) Total effects may be compared to assess the relative causal contributions of two or more variables. In the example, Z_1 has a greater effect on Z_4 than does Z_2 if and only if:

$$d_{41} + d_{43}d_{31} > d_{42} + d_{43}d_{32} \tag{5.13}$$

This conclusion depends on the validity of all assumptions made in the model and during the analysis, including the causal specification. Note that if only the multiple regression coefficients of Z_4 on Z_1 and Z_2 were used to assess degrees of causation, indirect effects would be ignored.

Analysis of Correlations

A second important result of path analysis is a formula that subdivides correlations into components and thereby makes possible a shortcut method for coefficient estimation.

Consider r_{14}, the correlation of Z_1 and Z_4. The correlation between any two variables is the expectation of the product of their standard scores:

$$r_{14} = E(Z_1 Z_4) \tag{5.14}$$

Substitute equation 5.11 for Z_4, multiply through by Z_1, and partition the expectation:

$$
\begin{aligned}
r_{14} = {} & (d_{41} + d_{43}d_{31})E(Z_1{}^2) \\
& + (d_{42} + d_{43}d_{32})E(Z_1 Z_2) \\
& + d_{43}d_{3c}E(Z_1 R_c{}') + d_{4d}E(Z_1 R_d{}').
\end{aligned} \tag{5.15}
$$

The third and fourth terms equal zero if we assume residuals are uncorrelated with exogenous variables. Using 5.14 plus the fact that $E(Z_i^2) = 1$, equation 5.15 can be rewritten as:

$$r_{14} = d_{41} + d_{43}d_{31} + d_{42}r_{12} + d_{43}d_{32}r_{12} \qquad (5.16)$$

Wright (1968 : 302) generalizes the result exemplified by 5.16 into an algorithm to use in conjunction with path diagrams:

> The correlation between any two variables in a properly constructed diagram of relations, which does not involve reciprocal interaction, is equal to the sum of contributions pertaining to the paths by which one may trace from one to the other without going back along any arrow after going forward along one, and without passing through any variable twice in the same path.

Note that Wright's rule holds only for recursive systems, and curved arrows are traced in applying it. Furthermore, as we have seen, the usual restriction on residuals is required to derive the formula.

If Wright's algorithm is applied to every possible correlation among variables in a recursive system, the resulting set of simultaneous equations can be solved to obtain path coefficients.[21]

Explained and Unexplained Variance

One final set of developments is needed for subsequent applications. These results concern the explanatory power both of individual variables and of entire theories. To obtain them it is easier to work from a model in which no variables intervene between exogenous variables and the outcome (figure 5.8).

21. In recursive systems, there are at most $n(n - 1)/2$ unknowns; and for any set of n variables, the same number of known empirical correlations exists. Thus a solution to the system of equations is guaranteed—the coefficients are identifiable. If fewer unknowns are sought, the system is overidentified. See the section below on path analytic causal inference.

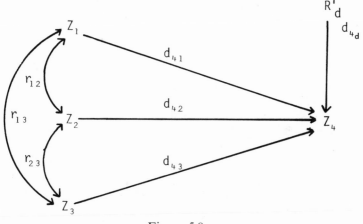

Figure 5.8

Results derived using this simple model are quite general.[22]
  Consider the correlation of Z_4 with itself:[23]

$$r_{44} = 1 = E(Z_4 \cdot Z_4) \tag{5.17}$$

Substitute for each Z_4 the basic equation for Z_4.

$$r_{44} = 1 = E[(d_{41}Z_1 + d_{42}Z_2 + d_{43}Z_3 + d_{4d}R_d')^2] \tag{5.18}$$

After calculating the square, rearranging terms, and substituting for expectations, we arrive at:

$$r_{44} = 1 = d_{41}{}^2 + d_{42}{}^2 + d_{43}{}^2 + 2d_{41}d_{42}r_{12}$$
$$+ 2d_{41}d_{43}r_{13} + 2d_{42}d_{43}r_{23} + d_{4d}{}^2 \tag{5.19}$$

22. More complex recursive models can be reduced to the two-stage form
    by applying these rules: (*a*) To eliminate variables in back of the preferred
    explanatory variables, use Wright's correlation algorithm. Thus remote
    links can be replaced by correlations between retained exogenous variables.
    (*b*) To eliminate intervening variables, employ the formula for a variable's
    total effect. Use total effect measures as path coefficients relating exogenous
    variables to the outcome.
23. This derivation generally follows Land (1969).

The results can be generalized:

$$r_{jj} = \sum_i d_j{}^2 + 2 \sum_{\substack{i,k \\ i \neq k}} d_{ji}d_{jk}r_{ik} + d_{jj}{}^2 = 1 \qquad (5.20)$$

In this formula, j is the outcome variable; i and k are indices running over all variables that directly affect j; and d_{jj} is the path coefficient from j's residual.

Since r_{jj} is equivalent to the variance of Z_j, equation 5.20 enables us to apportion $s_j{}^2$ into explained and unexplained components. Specifically, $d_{jj}{}^2$ measures *the variance* of Z_j *not explained by the explicit variables*; and $(1 - d_{jj}{}^2)$ measures the *variance explained* by the causal scheme.

In the important special case where all exogenous variables are uncorrelated with each other, equation 5.20 reduces to:

$$s_j{}^2 = 1 = \sum_i d_{ji}{}^2 + d_{jj}{}^2 \qquad (5.21)$$

Given this assumption of uncorrelated exogenous variables, the *squared path coefficient*, $d_{ji}{}^2$, directly measures the proportion of the total variance of Z_j explained by Z_i.

When exogenous variables are correlated, the total variance must be partitioned into three components: (*a*) unexplained variance—$d_{jj}{}^2$; (*b*) variance explained directly by each exogenous variable—the $d_{ji}{}^2$ terms; and (*c*) variance explained *jointly* by pairs of exogenous variables—the $2d_{ji}d_{jk}r_{ik}$ terms.

REVIEW AND MODIFICATION OF ASSUMPTIONS

This section lists, and briefly comments upon, key assumptions employed in path analysis.[24] There are three reasons for doing so: (*a*) to give additional emphasis to assumptions already mentioned less formally; (*b*) to make explicit assumptions not yet discussed; and (*c*) to sketch relaxations utilized in later chapters.

24. The section relies heavily on Heise (1969).

The Causal Specification

All path coefficient estimates are entirely relative to the hypothesized causal structure. Path regressions, path coefficients, and squared path coefficients measure causal effects only if the causal relations specified in the model are correct. If they are not, the estimation procedures yield mere "numerical nonsense," in Heise's phrase.

Recursiveness

As we have noted, identification is sometimes possible even when structural equations include reciprocal links; but the assumption of recursiveness is temptingly advantageous. Furthermore, certain results of path analysis, unless modified, apply only to recursive systems. Examples are Wright's algorithm for tracing correlations and the variance-apportioning formula (equation 5.20). Nevertheless, it will be necessary to consider nonrecursive systems in analyzing reciprocal power relations (chapter 9).

Uncorrelated Residuals

It is possible to identify coefficients without assuming uncorrelated residuals if enough coefficients can be declared zero or otherwise specified in advance. For most models, however, the assumption of uncorrelated residuals is essential. Furthermore, it is required to derive most of the path analysis results presented earlier. The restriction on disturbances is often more difficult to justify than any other assumption. Generally, it is only supported negatively—by inability to propose additional variables that might link error terms of different equations.

Linearity

Nonlinear relations can often be incorporated into a linear analysis, either by transforming the data, or by representing higher-power terms as "new" variables. For example, the multiplicative or interaction relation:

$$Y = X_1{}^a X_2{}^b \tag{5.22}$$

can be transformed to the additive relation:

$$\log Y = a \log X_1 + b \log X_2 \tag{5.23}$$

The second-degree equation:

$$Y = a_1 X_1 + a_2 X_1{}^2 \tag{5.24}$$

can be replaced by the first-degree equation:

$$Y = a_1 X_1 + a_2 X_2 \tag{5.25}$$

in which $X_2 = X_1{}^2$. Such devices may lead to complications in estimating parameters, but the researcher should be aware that nonlinear terms cannot be ruled out unless tests have been made for them.[25]

Measurement Assumptions

All derivations presented in this chapter assume variables measured on *interval* scales. In the nonexperimental social sciences, measurement at this level is often difficult or impossible,[26] a fact that led Dahl (1968) to be pessimistic about the use of causal inference methods in studying power. Path analysis, however, has broader applicability.

Boudon (1967:51–77, 104–107; 1968:216–20) has derived the principal theorems of path analysis, including Wright's rule for analyzing correlations, for systems of dichotomous variables. Chapter 6 applies Boudon's results to bring Dahl's

25. Cf. Alker's principle of minimal statistical constraint: "nonadditive causal modeling [is] in practice to be preferred to linear ... approaches, not so as to violate parsimony but so as to discover when simpler linear assumptions are in fact valid" (Alker, 1969:297). The problem is to know which nonlinear forms to test. Deductive theory can help one decide. For examples, see Przeworski and Soares (1971) or Nagel (1974).
26. The economists' controversy over the existence of a cardinal utility measure is particularly pertinent to the analysis of power as I define it. A cardinal utility is an interval measure of preferences.

and other existing power measures within the path analytic framework.

The appropriateness of path analysis for ordinal data remains a major unsettled issue. Labovitz (1970) shows that randomly generated ordinal transformations of one set of data do not greatly affect the value of bivariate standardized path coefficients (correlations), though the transformations do make unstandardized regressions unstable. He infers that ordinal variables can be treated as if they were interval variables. Boyle (1970), hoping to encourage the use of path analysis with ordinal data, argues that "regression and path coefficients are generally quite stable no matter what the [assumed] interval scale, because appreciable distortion depends" on improbable coincidences. He introduces a technique for decomposing ordinal variables into sets of dichotomous dummy variables and shows how it affords a check for coefficient stability under two different scale assumptions.

Wilson (1971), disputing Labovitz and Boyle, produces counterexamples where certain ordinal transformations preclude reliable inferences about causal structure and the magnitude of coefficients. Doubting the logical appropriateness of using ordinal variables in substantive theories, he advocates giving research priority to developing valid interval measures.

The controversy is not one I can resolve, though the use of path analysis with ordinal data is obviously an appealing possibility. An answer is not crucial for the primarily heuristic applications of path analysis in this book, since even Wilson agrees that "although ... interval-level techniques cannot be taken literally when applied to ordinal data, they can ... perform an important heuristic and metaphorical function in the interpretation of social phenomena." Those who would apply path analysis in empirical power research, however, must take the level of measurement problem into account.[27]

27. Additional discussions of ordinal data analysis may be found in Tufte (1969), Theil (1970), Hawkes (1970), Werts and Linn (1971, 1972), Lyons and Carter (1971), Lyons (1971), and Boyle (1971).

One additional point about measurement deserves emphasis: If path coefficients are to be treated seriously, it is necessary that the measures from which they are derived be highly reliable.[28] Techniques that correct for unreliable measures are possible (Heise, 1969; Blalock, 1970); but they considerably complicate the analysis.

Absence of Multicollinearity

In path analysis, exogenous variables are normally assumed to be correlated with each other. If these correlations are excessively large, however, it becomes difficult or impossible to estimate the separate effects of the correlated variables. Economists call this the problem of *multicollinearity* (Johnston, 1963: 201–07). As a correlation between explanatory variables grows, the standard error of estimate of the coefficients becomes progressively higher. Consequently, parameter estimates can vary widely with slight changes in the data and are less and less likely to satisfy significance tests.[29] In chapter 10, we shall see that the concept of multicollinearity has important implications in power analysis.

CAUSAL INFERENCES USING PATH ANALYSIS

The potential use of path analysis not only to *measure* but also to *infer* causality is one of its most exciting features. Enthusiasm should be tempered, however, for the method is easily subject to misinterpretation and abuse;[30] and it usually permits only limited, cautious conclusions.

Path analysis offers opportunities to make nonexperimental causal inferences through theory trimming and the use of "excess" equations to test between models.

28. Labovitz' evidence does not contradict this. His transformations all correlate above .90.
29. Multicollinearity is especially troublesome in models with interaction terms (Althauser, 1971; Gordon, 1968).
30. See Forbes and Tufte (1968) for examples.

Theory Trimming

The procedure known as theory trimming can be employed in two different ways: (a) When one is highly confident that the causal ordering in a model is correct, then a near-zero path coefficient between two variables permits the inference that those variables are not causally related. (b) When a model is regarded more tentatively, discovery of a near-zero path permits one to consider the model inferior to another model identical to it except for deletion of that path.

Both types of inference can be illustrated by figure 5.6, a structure used in previous derivations. If the data yield an estimate for d_{32} that differs insignificantly from zero, then figure 5.6 can be replaced by figure 5.9, in which the path from Z_2 to Z_3 is deleted.

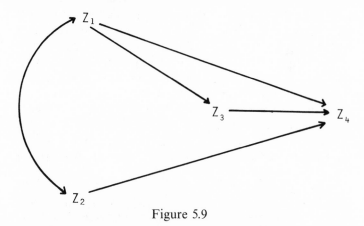

Figure 5.9

The difference concerns the nature of the conclusion drawn. In the first case (a), confidence in the entire structure permits one to infer that variables Z_2 and Z_3 are causally unrelated. In the second case (b), one should conclude only that the second *model* is better supported than the first. No firm conclusion concerning the Z_2–Z_3 relation is justified, because quite different models might yield non-zero coefficients between the two variables, and one is not sufficiently confident of the entire structure to rule out those alternatives.[31]

A difficulty in theory trimming is how to decide whether or not a slight difference from zero is "insignificant." Heise (1969) questions the value of conventional significance tests, claiming that they trim excessively large coefficients when samples are small and retain excessively small coefficients when samples are large. He suggests the criterion that any deletions should not affect the ability of the structure to reproduce the correlation matrix.[32] This merges theory trimming with our second causal inference method.

Test Based on Overidentification

Wright's algorithm generates equations relating every empirical correlation to the unknown path coefficients.[33] For an n-variable model, $n(n - 1)/2$ equations will be generated, one for every logically possible correlation. If one or more path coefficients can be specified zero a priori, then the number of equations exceeds the number of unknown coefficients.[34] Such a system is said to be "overidentified," since only one equation per unknown is required to identify the parameters by simultaneous solution.

Because all the equations are equally valid, those not used to solve for coefficients can be employed as a check on errors,

31. For an example, see the contrasting results for Models III–IIIA and Model IV in chapter 8 below.
32. Heise's criterion, however, merely shifts the significance testing problem from the difference between the coefficient and zero to the difference between test and empirical correlations.

    Haitovsky (1969) shows for conventional regression that to maximize $\bar{R}^2$ (the proportion of variance explained, corrected for degrees of freedom), one should retain all coefficients with t statistics greater than one (a standard often less strict than conventional significance cutoff levels). I suspect that this criterion, applied at each stage of a recursive path model, would satisfy Heise's desideratum as well.
33. The same equations can be generated by a matrix algebra procedure suggested by Boudon (1965, 1967, 1968).
34. Zero path coefficients between exogenous variables do not count, however. The only equations they yield are identities of the type $r_{ij} = r_{ij}$.

including errors resulting from incorrect causal specification. Which equations should be used in estimation and which in testing? Equations for correlations between variables that are *directly* related in the causal scheme are identical with the normal equations of least squares regression. Goldberger (1970) has shown that least squares gives the most efficient estimate of the parameters in recursive systems (assuming uncorrelated residuals). Therefore, equations involving these correlations should be used for estimation. A test equation will remain for each potential path omitted from the specification.[35]

Unlike theory trimming, the method of test equations permits inferences concerning the *direction* of causation. Suppose we wish to test between Model I, in which X_3 causes X_4, and Model II, in which X_4 causes X_3 (see figure 5.10).

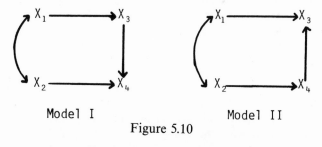

Model I   Model II

Figure 5.10

There are six possible correlations, but the equation for r_{12} yields only an identity. There are three path coefficients to estimate. Because d_{41} and d_{32} are specified zero a priori in both models, equations for correlations between these two

---

35. Boudon, not realizing the greater efficiency of ordinary regression, proposed that *all* correlation equations be used in estimating coefficients. He resolved the problem of over-identification by a special least squares computation, which yields coefficients having the closest fit to the entire set of equations. This procedure permits use of all correlation equations to test the model, except for any that belong to just-identified subsystems (a qualification Boudon failed to point out). See Boudon (1965; 1967: 101–04; and 1968: 211–15) and Goldberger (1970).

variable pairs are available to test between the models. Estimating equations for Model I are:

$$r_{13} = d_{31} \tag{5.26a}$$

$$r_{24} = r_{12}d_{31}d_{43} + d_{42} \tag{5.26b}$$

$$r_{34} = d_{43} + d_{31}r_{12}d_{42} \tag{5.26c}$$

These equations can be easily solved, given the empirical correlations.

Estimating equations for Model II are obtained in similar fashion:

$$r_{13} = d_{31} + r_{12}d_{42}d_{34} \tag{5.27a}$$

$$r_{24} = d_{42} \tag{5.27b}$$

$$r_{34} = d_{31}r_{12}d_{42} + d_{34} \tag{5.27c}$$

Notice how the two sets of equations differ. They will normally yield conflicting estimates for *all* parameters, even though the two structures disagree over only one link.

Test equations for Model I are:

$$r_{14} = d_{31}d_{43} + r_{12}d_{42} \tag{5.28a}$$

$$r_{23} = r_{12}d_{31} \tag{5.28b}$$

Estimates for d_{31}, d_{43}, and d_{42}, together with the known value of r_{12}, are substituted in these test equations; and the results are compared with the known values of r_{14} and r_{23}.[36] A similar procedure is followed for Model II, which is tested by the following equations:

$$r_{14} = r_{12}d_{42} \tag{5.29a}$$

$$r_{23} = r_{12}d_{31} + d_{42}d_{34} \tag{5.29b}$$

If parameters for a model do not fit all its test equations reasonably well, then that model should be rejected. It is

36. Test equations used in the Simon-Blalock causal inference method are equivalent to those derived from path analysis. For a demonstration, see Nagel (1972:132–33) and for comments on relations between the methods, see Blalock (1971:73–74). Because it leads directly to parameter estimates, path analysis is preferable to the Simon–Blalock method.

quite possible, however, that both models or neither model will provide a good match to the test equations. Tests based on overidentification do not guarantee an easy choice of one model over another.

Even clear-cut superiority of one model over others with which it is compared does not prove its validity. First, even when several theories are tested, numerous alternatives remain, any one of which might be preferable to the best tested model. Besides the two models in figure 5.10, there exist 4094 other logically possible models constructed from the same four variables![37] Furthermore, better theories might be constructed by incorporating additional variables, which would increase the number of possible models even more fantastically. Thus, the testing procedure advances theory only by eliminating less adequate models. Progress depends primarily on the ability of researchers to imagine plausible models and to exclude possible combinations a priori.

A second caveat must be mentioned. The closer a structure approaches to being just-identified, the more likely it is to satisfy its test equations. Therefore, the confidence vested in any theory that fits its test equations should vary directly with the number of possible links specified zero in advance (Blalock, 1970). Conversely, "improvements" in fit gained by adding links may be artifacts resulting from closer approximation of the model to a complete recursive system (Heise, 1969).

The caution with which one should regard causal inferences derived from path analysis is demonstrated in chapter 8, where data from research on constituency influence in Congress are subjected to path analysis. Both theory trimming and test equations are used to show that path analysis can produce some theoretical progress even when it does not lead to unambiguous conclusions.

37. Each of the $n(n - 1)/2$ pairs of variables may be related in any of four different ways—X_1 causes X_2; X_2 causes X_1; X_1 and X_2 reciprocally affect each other; or there is no connection between X_1 and X_2. There are $4^{n(n - 1)/2}$ possible combinations of the pair-wise relations.

PART II: APPLICATIONS

6 MEASURES OF POWER

The preceding five chapters introduced the basic ideas upon which this book depends: the concepts of preference and causal ordering, the definition of power as a causal relation between preferences and outcomes, and path analysis as a method of measuring and inferring causation. The remaining chapters attempt to show that both the conceptual understanding and the empirical study of power can be advanced by building upon these foundations.

The present chapter deals with numerical measures of power. Its first section proposes that coefficients from path analysis be used to measure power, points out complications in applying them, and discusses their limitations and advantages. The second section relates path measures of power to well-known measures proposed by Dahl, March, and Shapley and Shubik.

Chapter 7 gives special attention to power that is exercised indirectly through control over the preferences of others. Suggestions about the use of path analysis in empirical power research and an illustration of the method are presented in chapter 8. Chapter 9 analyzes reciprocal power relations and shows how to treat them within the asymmetric causal framework. Chapter 10 shows how power in a system can expand or contract and traces relations between power, conflict, and benefit. The final chapter points out the intersection between descriptive analysis and explanatory theory and then assesses the usefulness of "power."

PATH ANALYTIC POWER MEASURES

The argument here is already obvious: If power relations are a subset of causal relations, then any measure of causation can measure power. Path analysis provides measures of causal effect. Therefore, coefficients from path analysis can measure power. Specifically, an actor's power over an outcome is indicated by appropriate path measures of the causal effect of his preferences on the outcome.

Choice of Coefficients

As chapter 5 shows, path analysis yields three coefficients— the path regression, the standardized path coefficient, and the squared path coefficient. In deciding conditions under which each is appropriate for power applications, we can draw on a more general debate over the relative merits of standardized and unstandardized coefficients.[1]

Algorithms of path analysis are simplest when expressed using Wright's standardized path coefficients.[2] Moreover, path coefficients do not vary with the scales that measure variables; and, like the correlation coefficient, the path coefficient seems easily understood, because it normally ranges between $+1$ and -1.[3] Finally, standardized variables permit treatment of residuals in the same form as measured variables (Wright, 1960).

Proponents of unstandardized coefficients argue that standardized coefficients are misleading, because they are adjusted for the amount of variation in the dependent variable. Therefore, even when underlying causal laws remain constant, as indicated by unvarying path regressions (which estimate the true structural coefficients), path coefficients can fluctuate from one study to another, if other variables or random events

1. Tukey (1954) broached the question by criticizing Wright's reliance on standardized coefficients. Turner and Stevens (1959) and Blalock (1967a, 1967b), echo his arguments. Wright (1960) has offered a balanced reply. Other contributions include Forbes and Tufte (1968b) and Tufte (1968).
2. But comparable formulas for, e.g., indirect and total effects can be written with path regressions. See Turner and Stevens (1959).
3. Path coefficients can exceed these limits when exogenous variables are negatively correlated.

cause differing standard deviations in the dependent variable.[4] In contrast, path regressions are more often stable and are therefore comparable across populations or across time for the same population.[5] Furthermore, the path regression affords a clearer substantive and predictive interpretation: If the coefficient is a_{ji}, then a unit change in X_i should result in a change of a_{ji} units in X_j. Finally, the path regression, as an estimate of the structural coefficient, can be inserted in the algebraic expression of the causal relation, where it may contribute to further theoretical developments.

Even critics of standardized coefficients recognize occasions where their use is unobjectionable: (a) when interest is restricted to one population and no comparisons across populations are made (Blalock, 1967b); (b) when independent and dependent variables have equal standard deviations, because the path coefficient and path regression are then equal (Tukey, 1954); (c) "when the measurement of one or both variables on a determinate scale is hopeless," because the units employed in one study cannot be proven to be the same as those in another (Tukey, 1954). Therefore the stability argument for the path regression breaks down.[6]

This last condition especially applies to power measurement, where variables representing preferences must function as a causal factor. The search for a "determinate scale" for measuring preferences (and attitudes generally) is a notoriously difficult problem for the social sciences.[7] Therefore, the path regression loses one of its chief advantages over the path

4. This possibility can be appreciated by studying the formula relating the two coefficients:

$$d_{ji} = a_{ji}(s_i/s_j)$$

5. Tukey (1954) gives conditions for stability of regression coefficients.

6. In fact, Labovitz' (1970) evidence suggests that in the extreme case of an indeterminate scale—purely ordinal data—standardized measures are *more* stable than unstandardized.

7. A "determinate scale" of preferences would be an interpersonally comparable cardinal utility.

coefficient,[8] and may indeed mislead a researcher who assumes that its use guarantees comparability across populations or time.

Instead, power measures will ordinarily be *not* comparable when based on two different populations or on the same population at different times, regardless of whether or not coefficients are standardized. Thus, if one measures the influence of American and Soviet military leaders on their nations' foreign policies and obtains path coefficients of .5 and .3, respectively, the inference that the U.S. military has more influence than its Soviet counterpart is not warranted. Internal comparisons would be appropriate, however, and from them one could draw conclusions about the relative positions of similar actors in the two systems (e.g., in the U.S., the military affects foreign policy more than does the State Department, whereas in the U.S.S.R. the foreign ministry dominates).

Finally, a word about the squared path coefficient is in order. This measure, of course, shares all drawbacks of the path coefficient. Under certain conditions, however, it possesses advantages of its own. If the exogenous variables are not correlated, the squared path coefficient d_{ji}^2 measures the proportion of variance in X_j accounted for by X_i (see equation 5.21). Therefore, when preferences are uncorrelated, the squared path coefficient can be treated as a ratio scale of power. An actor whose power is measured by a squared coefficient of .8 would then, in a meaningful sense, have twice as much influence as one whose squared measure is .4; whereas an unsquared path coefficient of .8 does not indicate twice as much power as does one of .4. Empirically, uncorrelated preferences occur rarely; the squared coefficient may nevertheless have an important application in the theoretical analysis of voting systems, a possibility explored later in this chapter.

8. Forbes and Tufte (1968b) use this point in refuting an argument made by Blalock (1967a) and by Cnudde and McCrone (1968) about the Miller–Stokes constituency influence study.

Power over Unique Events

In measuring power, it is important to distinguish between the causal measure of an actor's power over an outcome variable and the power the actor exercises over any one event within the outcome category.[9] The causal measure is given by the appropriate path regression or path coefficient and should be derived from repeated observations of outcomes and preferences. The actor's effect on a unique occurrence, in contrast, depends on both his general power and on the direction and intensity of his preference concerning that particular event. This distinction can be seen more clearly by examining a two-person path equation:[10]

$$Y_3 = d_{31}U_1 + d_{32}U_2 + d_{3c}R_c \tag{6.1}$$

If actor 1 has no preference regarding a particular instance of Y_3 (i.e., $U_1 = 0$), his effect on Y_3 in that case will be nil, no matter what the value of d_{31}. Similarly, even if d_{31} exceeds d_{32} and d_{3c}, in any given case the effect of actor 1, $d_{31}U_1$, may be outweighed if actor 2 has an especially intense preference or if disturbances are unusually important.

In construing an actor's effect on an outcome as the product of power and preference, our equations represent mathematically the assumption of commonsense psychology that personal causality depends on both ability—*A can* do *Y*—and on motivation—*A wants* to do *Y* (Heider, 1958:chapter 4). Debates in the community power literature reflect a similar premise, as when Bachrach and Baratz (1962) criticize Dahl (1961) for studying outcomes about which a putative elite had no strong preferences.

9. This section was inspired by a similar, but more general discussion in Blalock (1968b:186–89). As Blalock puts it, "One must learn to distinguish ... between *causal laws* that presumably hold true in general or under certain specified conditions and *causes* that are operating in any given case."

10. For easier interpretation of this and subsequent equations, I replace *Z*'s by my original *Y*, *X*, and *U* notation. Variables are assumed standardized whenever accompanied by path coefficients.

Methodologically, this analysis implies two prescriptions: First, in selecting events for observation in a power study, one should include a wide range of preference intensities for each actor whose power is to be gauged. Second, one should be wary of inferring power or shifts in power from a few events. If an outcome pattern changes, it may not mean that a new group has come to power, but that an old elite has changed preferences. Or, if a supposed elite's known preferences fail to dominate, the result may be due less to loss of power than to an unusual configuration of preference intensities.

Measures of Nonlinear Power

Not only do path coefficients and preferences interact in determining specific events, but they also mutually determine *measures* of power in nonlinear systems. When a linear structure best predicts the outcome, the path coefficient (or path regression) measures power. When an actor's preferences are nonlinearly related to outcomes, however, the coefficient alone no longer appropriately measures power. Instead, the partial derivative of the outcome variable with respect to the actor's preference variable provides a better measure.[11] In general, the preference will be a factor in this quantity. Consider a two-actor system where outcome Y_3 varies as the square of actor 2's preference:

$$Y_3 = d_{31}U_1 + d_{32}U_2{}^2 \tag{6.2}$$

The partial derivative of Y_3 with respect to U_2 is $d_{32}U_2$: the more intensely 2 cares about the outcome, the greater her power. Her effect, as equation 6.2 indicates, rises more than proportionately as her degree of concern increases. In a democracy, for example, an impassioned majority may overwhelm special interests, though the latter get their way in ordinary circumstances.

11. The path coefficient *is* the partial derivative in the linear case (if variables are standardized).

Intervening Variables and Multiple Paths of Influence

A great virtue of path measures is their ability to assess influence exercised through intervening variables.

For a simple influence chain, $U_1 \rightarrow X_2 \rightarrow Y_3$, the natural power measure based on the path coefficient is the compound path coefficient, $d_{321} = d_{32}d_{21}$ (equation 5.12). The squared compound path coefficient is elementary: $d_{321}^2 = d_{32}^2 d_{21}^2$. When unstandardized path regressions are used, conversion requires correction for only the first and last variables in the chain: $a_{321} = d_{321}(s_3/s_1)$.[12] If path regressions are calculated separately, their product is the compound path regression relating the two variables at either end of the chain (Tukey, 1954).

For multiple paths of influence, the logical measure of an actor's power is the path measure of the total effect of his preference upon the outcome—the sum of all path coefficients, simple or compound, connecting the two variables.[13] Similarly, the regression measure is the sum of the path regressions across the same paths. The squared path coefficient measure for the multiple-path case is the square of the path coefficient total effect measure (figure 6.1).

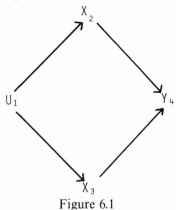

Figure 6.1

12. Standard deviations of intervening variables cancel out.
13. See the section on indirect and total effects in chapter 5 above.

For the model in figure 6.1, this quantity is:

$$(d_{21}d_{42} + d_{31}d_{43})^2 = d_{21}{}^2d_{42}{}^2 + 2d_{21}d_{42}d_{31}d_{43}$$
$$+ d_{31}{}^2d_{43}{}^2 \qquad (6.3)$$

An especially important type of influence exercised indirectly occurs when the intervening variable is the preference of another actor. Because this pattern is so significant empirically, and because it gives rise to intriguing difficulties, all of chapter 7 is devoted to it.

Limitations and Advantages of Path Measures of Power

The chief limitations of path analytic power measures are imposed by the necessary assumptions of path analysis. Since they have been stressed in chapter 5, there is no need to repeat them. It is worth noting, however, that one advantage of applying path methods to power measurement is that the researcher then knows (or should know) and can make explicit such assumptions, which are too often ignored in conventional studies.

Path measures of power are outcome-specific. They do not measure power as a generalized capacity but instead apportion influence over a specified dependent variable. Thus each path model of power requires a set of events or outcomes that can be meaningfully treated as a single variable. Path measures can, however, be used to develop theories of power, from which indices of power as a generalized capacity might be derived. This topic will be treated in chapter 11.

Numerous benefits flow from assimilating power measurement to standard statistical methodology; only a few will be mentioned here. Path methods make it possible to: (*a*) measure the influence of more than one actor over an outcome variable; (*b*) assess influence exercised via intermediaries and through several paths; (*c*) incorporate variables other than preferences and outcomes, so that refined understanding of influence can be developed; (*d*) tie power measurement to a method of causal inference and therefore permit inferences concerning the existence and direction of power; (*e*) use at least two levels of measurement—nominal and interval—and possibly ordinal as well; (*f*) measure power in large systems over numerous separate events or outcomes.

These practical virtues of path measures argue strongly for their adoption in empirical power research; but the path analytic framework can also be justified by its ability to assist in solving conceptual and theoretical questions. The rest of this chapter and most of the remaining chapters substantiate this claim.

RELATION OF PATH MEASURES TO OTHER MEASURES OF POWER

If the measurement proposals in the preceding section are to reduce, rather than compound confusion in power analysis, it is necessary to relate them to existing power measures.

Rather than attempt the impossible task of connecting path measures to all, or even a fair sample of, the "power measures" in the literature, I examine only those of Dahl (1957), March (1957), and Shapley and Shubik (1954). These three have been chosen for a number of reasons: (*a*) They are widely cited and influential. (*b*) They are not ad hoc indices designed for specific studies but instead are theoretically grounded and intended to have wide applicability. (*c*) They attempt to assess the root idea of power, not constructs derived from it.[14] (*d*) Finally, these three, along with two others, were examined by Riker (1964:343), who saw "no possible equation" among them. Riker despaired of finding "a yet more general formulation which combines these . . . neatly into one." If our framework can suggest an underlying unity, it may reduce pessimism and bewilderment concerning the concept of power.

14. Excluded by one or more of these criteria are, among others, the reputational indices of Hunter (1953); the structural measures of Brams (1968), Russett (1968), and Mayhew, Gray, and Richardson (1969); and the forty-five (!) "operational definitions" of "power" factor-analyzed by Barber (1966).

In analyzing the three measures, we distinguish between their *formal* structures and the *interpretation* their authors give to the variables they employ. For reasons argued at length in chapters 2 and 3, I disagree with Dahl and March over the classes of causes and effects to use in defining power. This difference, however, does not preclude comparison of mathematical structures in order to seek formal similarities.

Dahl's Amount of Power

Much recent work on power takes as its starting point Dahl's concept of the *amount* of power.[15] This measure is defined for power relations between two actors. Actor 1, wishing 2 to perform an act Y, tries to induce 2's compliance by performing some influence attempt or preference communication, W. The amount of power, M, is defined as the difference between the conditional probabilities of 2's performing Y with and without 1's intervention:[16]

$$M = P(Y_2|W_1) - P(Y_2|\overline{W}_1) \tag{6.4}$$

The probabilities can be flexibly interpreted as empirical relative frequencies (Dahl, 1957; Gamson, 1968), consciously adopted mixed strategies (Harsanyi, 1962a), or personal probabilities of informed observers.

Dahl's measure reflects a behaviorist conception of power, since 1's action, W_1, must precede compliance by 2. According to my definition, the causal variable in power should be preferences, not behavior. Therefore, I shall replace Dahl's causal variable W_1 with U_1, 1's preference concerning 2's action. This change would be important in substantive interpretations of the formula, but the mathematics remains the same whether W_1 or U_1 is used.

Considered causally, Dahl's power situation is the most elementary case (see figure 4.2). Dahl's variables are also the

15. For example, Harsanyi (1962a, 1962b), Tannenbaum (1962), and Gamson (1968).
16. Dahl's notation has been modified to make it more consistent with usage in this book.

simplest possible. Both preferences and outcomes are dichotomous. As I noted in chapter 5, Boudon has shown that the principal results of path analysis apply to variables measured at this level.

In two-variable structures of this type, the path coefficient is the correlation coefficient for dichotomous variables, ϕ:

$$d_{21} = \phi_{12} = \frac{P_{12} - P_1 P_2}{\sqrt{[P_1(1 - P_1)P_2(1 - P_2)]}} \tag{6.5}$$

In equation 6.5, P_{12} is the probability that both U_1 and Y_2 are true; P_1 is the probability that U_1 alone is true; and P_2 is the probability of Y_2 alone (Alker, 1965:81).

Now consider Dahl's amount of power (equation 6.4). Substitute for his conditional probabilities their equivalents in joint and simple probabilities:

$$M = \frac{P_{12}}{P_1} - \frac{P_{\bar{1}2}}{P_{\bar{1}}} \tag{6.6}$$

Substitute for $P_{\bar{1}2}$ and $P_{\bar{1}}$, and then cross multiply to achieve a common denominator:

$$M = \frac{P_{12}(1 - P_1) - (P_2 - P_{12})P_1}{P_1(1 - P_1)} \tag{6.7}$$

Equation 6.7 simplifies to:

$$M = \frac{P_{12} - P_1 P_2}{P_1(1 - P_1)} \tag{6.8}$$

Equations 6.8 and 6.5 differ only in their denominators. But for dichotomous variables, $s_i = \sqrt{[P_i(1 - P_i)]}$ (Alker, 1965:81). Therefore, the path coefficient is related to Dahl's amount of power by the expression:

$$d_{21} = M(s_1/s_2) \tag{6.9}$$

But this is exactly the relation between the path coefficient and the path regression (see equation 5.8).[17]

17. Similar proofs, though without reference to Dahl's power measure, are given by Alker (1965:80–85) and Boudon (1967:69).

   Thus, formally, Dahl's amount of power is the path regression coefficient for the special case in which (*a*) only a single actor's preference has causal effect; and (*b*) both preference and outcome are dichotomous. Therefore, except for interpretative differences, Dahl's power measure and analysis can be subsumed within the path analytic approach to power.

March's Measurement Concept

   Another noteworthy attempt to develop a theoretically informed influence measure is that of March (1957). Like Dahl, March employs key terms that differ from those I advocate. He uses "roles" in place of "actor," and "behavior" instead of "preference" as the causal variable. As with Dahl, these discrepancies can be treated as questions of interpretation, for they do not affect formal properties.

   March does not attempt to develop a single numerical influence measure. Instead, he proposes a general criterion for *ranking* the influence of roles and behaviors: "By 'more influential' we want to mean the role that, in some sense, is more successful than the other at narrowing the range of possible outcomes." March does not, however, use "range" in its statistical sense. He means only that, given the choice of behavior by the role-incumbent, the set of outcomes becomes "smaller" with respect to a "measure" on the outcomes. Although he sketches two broad classes of possible measures, March imposes no formal restriction on the idea, leaving its interpretation to researchers engaged in specific studies.

   Path measures satisfy March's criterion. For an actor to have influence according to these measures, knowledge of the actor's preference must reduce unexplained outcome variance. This residual variance satisfactorily fits what March seems to mean by a "measure" on outcomes.

   When exogenous variables are uncorrelated, a measure of variance not explained by preference U_i is $(1 - d_{ji}^2)$, where Y_j is the outcome variable (equation 5.21).[18] When causal

18. Compare the sample variance of estimate (squared coefficient of alienation) for simple bivariate regression (Hays, 1963: 498; Blalock, 1960: 295–99).

variables are correlated, measures of variance unexplained by U_i are ambiguous, but nevertheless always inversely related to the path coefficient (equation 5.20).

Thus March's approach to power measurement is the *complement* of the influence coefficient approach. His "measure" on the outcomes *decreases* as the actor's influence *increases*; and his influence ranking criterion stipulates that a role has *more* influence than another if the "measure" given its behavior is *less* than the measure given the other's.

Strictly speaking, path measures are a subset of all the influence measuring and ordering devices compatible with March's criterion. His concept of a "measure on the outcomes" is extremely general; the unexplained variance is only one of many conceivable interpretations. Thus, whereas Dahl's power measure is a special case of the path measurement approach, the latter in turn is a special case of March's criterion.[19]

The generality of March's criterion entails lack of operational specificity. Perhaps as a result, the criterion has never, so far as I know, been used in an empirical power study. When March does give an example of his analysis (in an appendix to his paper), he resorts to a linear additive model of the type Boudon (1967: chapter 2) uses to derive path algorithms for dichotomous variables. March's model includes "coefficients of influence," but he neglects them to focus on his ranking criterion. The coefficients are, in fact, of the same type as Dahl's M, except that March's model has two independent variables, whereas Dahl uses only one. Thus March's *example* fits within the class of power models and measures developed in this book.

19. In other respects, however, March's criterion is *less* general than the measures developed in this book. March's key variables are "role" and "behavior," rather than the more general "actor" and "preference." Furthermore, March insists that role R_1 be considered more influential than role R_2 only if R_1 is more influential than R_2 with respect to *each* behavior in a specified set. Regression measures, in contrast, sum over all values of the independent variable. While there may be instances in which one wants to compare the influence of two actors with respect to a single behavior (or preference) regarding an outcome, March's requirement seems unduly restrictive for comparing the *overall* influence of two or more actors with respect to an outcome variable.

The Shapley–Shubik Voting Power Index[20]

The power index of Shapley and Shubik (1954) is both the most limited and the most practical of the three measurement concepts considered in this chapter. The purpose of the index is to measure the power that actors in a voting system receive from its formal rules alone, specifically, from the votes assigned to each actor and the votes required for victory. When votes are apportioned unequally, what we intuitively think of as power may deviate strongly and in nonobvious ways from numerical vote assignments. The Shapley–Shubik index gives a convincing assessment of a priori voting strength for systems of this type, a category which includes the U.N. Security Council, the U.S. Electoral College, and corporation stock-holders' meetings.

The formula for the index seems intimidating at first:[21]

$$\phi_i = \sum_{S \ni i} \frac{(s-1)!(n-s)!}{n!} v(S) - \sum_{S \not\ni i} \frac{s!(n-s-1)!}{n!} v(S)$$

$$(6.10)$$

The symbols have the following meanings:

ϕ_i = the power index for voter i[22]

S = an index running across all possible voting coalitions (combinations of voters)

$S \ni i$ = coalitions that include i

$S \not\ni i$ = coalitions that do not include i

s = the number of members in S

n = the number of voters in the system

$v(S)$ = 1 if S is a winning coalition

0 if S is not a winning coalition

---

20. I am grateful to Michael Allingham and Donald Fujihira for their interest in this problem. Most of the results presented here are due to their efforts.
21. There exist several other equivalent versions.
22. The ϕ used by Shapley and Shubik should not be confused with the correlation coefficient employed above in relating Dahl's M to path measures of power.

Shapley and Shubik suggest that their formula be interpreted as the a priori probability that i will cast the decisive (or "pivotal") vote on any issue, assuming all possible voting sequences (permutations of the n voters) are equally likely. They stress, however, that other interpretations might be compatible with the formula. In fact, the index is a special application of the Shapley value for n-person games, which in turn was derived mathematically from three highly abstract axioms (Shapley, 1953).

To relate the Shapley–Shubik index to path measures, let us analyze the voting situation from a causal perspective. The obvious causal events are the votes of each actor. We can reasonably assume they represent the actor's preferences. The outcome events are collective decisions about bills, motions, or other proposals. Each causal event can have two states—a yes vote or a no vote. Each outcome event likewise has two possible states—passage or rejection. If we imagine a large series of votes, the elementary causal and outcome events can be aggregated into the probability (relative frequency) of, respectively, yes votes by each individual and affirmative decisions by the collectivity.

Our purpose is to measure statistically the degree of causal effect of the first variable on the second. In an a priori analysis, this can be done once we derive the structural equation relating the two variables. We start with the identity

$$P(W) = \sum_{S} P(S)v(S) \tag{6.11}$$

$P(W)$ is the probability that a bill will pass; $P(S)$ is the probability that voting coalition S (a combination of the voters) will form, where S is any coalition that favors passage; and $v(S)$, as in the Shapley–Shubik formula, equals 1 if S is a winning coalition and 0 if S is not winning.

To derive $P(W)$ from individual votes, we follow the Shapley–Shubik assumption that voters' preferences are uncorrelated. It is then possible to substitute for $P(S)$ as follows:

$$P(W) = \sum_S \prod_{j \in S} P(j) \prod_{k \notin S} [1 - P(k)]v(S), \qquad (6.12)$$

where j and k are individual voters, and $P(j)$ and $P(k)$ are the probabilities of their voting yes.

Now that we have related $P(W)$ to individual propensities to favor passage, we can phrase our causal query as follows: "How much more (or less) frequently will affirmative decisions occur if voter i increases (or decreases) the probability that he will vote yes by a given amount?" The path regression gives a numerical answer to this question. Because equation 6.12 is nonlinear, however, the path regression is not automatically obtained from the formula. Instead, we must evaluate the partial derivative of $P(W)$ with respect to $P(i)$, assuming that all the other $P(j)$ and $P(k)$ are held constant while $P(i)$ changes marginally. Allingham (1973) and Fujihira (1974) have both shown that this operation yields:

$$\frac{\partial P(W)}{\partial P(i)} = \frac{1}{2^{n-1}} \left[\sum_{S \ni i} v(S) - \sum_{S \not\ni i} v(S) \right] \qquad (6.13)$$

Allingham has also proved that 6.13 is equivalent to the Dahl amount of power. This equivalence is, of course, implied by my earlier demonstration that the Dahl measure and the path regression are the same.

As Allingham observes, 6.13 "is simply the Shapley value [equation 6.10] without the weights." He shows that the two formulas are not numerically equivalent, but they are weakly ordinally equivalent. That is, if actor j has more power than actor k according to the Shapley–Shubik index, she will not have less power than k according to the path regression, and vice versa.

By resort to authority rather than formal proof, it is possible to emphasize more strongly the compatibility of the two measures. Allingham has further proved that 6.13 is the Banzhaf measure of voting power, an index which Banzhaf, a lawyer, has applied with significant legal impact in controversies over weighted voting, multimember electoral districts, and the Electoral College.[23] In support of one of Banzhaf's suits, Shapley, Riker, and other experts submitted affidavits stating that the Banzhaf method is "both consistent with and a reasonable extension of the generally recognized techniques for the measurement of voting power" (i.e., the Shapley–Shubik index).[24]

I conclude then that path measures of voting power are closely and compatibly related to the Shapley–Shubik index. Nevertheless, it is disappointing that we lack proof of a relation of strict equivalence, because ordinally equivalent measures will not resolve all practical disputes. If, for example, a court should order that voting "power" be apportioned among districts in exact proportion to their populations, the Shapley value and the path regression would generally give different apportionments.

It may be that the squared path coefficient is equivalent to the Shapley–Shubik index. Like the Shapley value, the squared coefficient is a ratio measure of power when preferences are uncorrelated (as we assume in a priori voting analysis). Furthermore, when there is no residual variance (also true in voting situations), the sum of voters' squared path coefficients

23. Banzhaf (1965, 1966, 1968). Banzhaf derived the measure from two assumptions: (a) that all voting *combinations* are equally likely; and (b) that a voter has power whenever he is "critical" to the success of a coalition (i.e., the coalition would change from winning to losing if he changes his vote). The Shapley–Shubik index assumes, in contrast, that (a) all *permutations* of voters are equally likely; and (b) a voter has power whenever he is "pivotal" (i.e., the last member to join a minimal winning coalition).

24. Banzhaf (1968: n. 8). Cf. also Riker and Shapley (1968: 204).

   In their original article, Shapley and Shubik (1954) stated that any proposed power measure for a voting system should give the same results as theirs or else lead to a "logical inconsistency." By this they meant the measure would conflict with one or more of Shapley's axioms. Shapley's more recent tolerant attitude may result from realization that one of his axioms (additivity) is not relevant to simple games (those with 1–0 outcomes). See Allingham (1973:3).

is one, as is the sum of the Shapley–Shubik indices. (The path regression must be specially normalized to sum to one.) Unfortunately, I must be content with conjecturing about this possible equivalence, for I have been unable to find a proof.

7 *INDIRECT INFLUENCE*

"Indirect influence" denotes a variety of processes. Some authors apply the term to any relation in which one actor controls another by using covert devices, as by screening information. Dahl (1961) uses indirect influence as a synonym for rule by anticipated reactions. From the causal perspective, we might term indirect any power model in which intervening variables appear between preferences and the outcome.

In this chapter, however, I confine indirect influence to sequences where the variable intervening between one actor's preference and the outcome is the preference of a second actor. Processes of this type are ubiquitous and important. They include such modes of influence as persuasion, indoctrination, and conditioning. By broadening power analysis to include causation of preferences by preferences, we heed scholars of the left (e.g., Balbus, 1971), who urge more attention to preference formation. At the same time, we remain perfectly consistent with our basic definition of power, because preferences are outcomes subject to causation, and other preferences may be among the variables causing them. Opening up influence analysis in this way clarifies several significant debates over the attribution of power.

PROXIMATE AND ULTIMATE POWER

The attention of the world normally focuses upon actors who exercise *proximate* power. Their decisions are the immediate causes of outcomes. Consequently, they become centers of communication networks, possessors of high status, objects of hope and fear for the multitudes.

Most truly important questions about political systems ask whether or not these actors possess *ultimate* power. It is not surprising to know that a chairman dominates his corporation, a mayor her city's government, a president his nation's foreign policy. What we really want to know is whether their desires function autonomously, or if they are shaped by the preferences of others. And, if the latter, which others? Does the executive respond to stockholders, workers, consumers, or government? Does the mayor heed voters or businessmen? Is the president dominated by generals, capitalists, intellectuals, the people?

This section first sketches a diagrammatic and statistical framework for posing such questions. Next, illustrations are presented clarifying the rival positions in debates about U.S. power structures. Conceptual limits to ultimate power are then described and applied to evaluate the power of visionaries, prophets, and historical villains.

Measures of Indirect and Autonomous Power

The most elementary case of indirect influence is diagrammed in figure 7.1 :

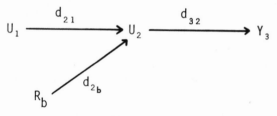

Figure 7.1

The direct or proximate power of actor 2 over Y_3 is measured by d_{32}. A portion of this control should, however, be attributed to actor 1, who exercises some degree of ultimate influence over Y_3. This portion is measured by the compound path coefficient $d_{21}d_{32}$.

What then is the true influence of actor 2? Certainly if her preferences are entirely determined by actor 1, then we should want to say she has no real power. But actor 1 may have only slight or moderate effect upon U_2. If so, part of the determination of Y_3 should be attributed to 2's "own" preferences. A reasonable solution is to treat the residual of U_2 as 2's *autonomous* preference.[1] After all, it cannot be attributed to anyone else unless other variables are brought into the model.

The effect of 2's autonomous preference on Y_3 is measured by the compound path coefficient from the residual to Y_3, $d_{2b}d_{32}$. This we shall adopt as the measure of 2's autonomous power over the outcome.[2] Ultimate power over Y_3 is thereby apportioned between actor 1 $(d_{21}d_{32})$ and actor 2 $(d_{2b}d_{32})$.

Conflicting Hypotheses about U.S. Power Structures

Power studies concerned with the degree of democracy in modern systems *must* deal with indirect influence. Since direct democracy is seldom feasible, decisions are normally made by elected leaders or by officials they appoint. Elections are intended to produce popular influence over officeholders, but their efficacy cannot be taken for granted. Consequently,

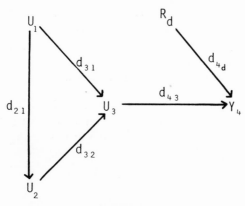

Figure 7.2

1. Use of this stratagem does not imply that nonautonomous preferences are insincere.
2. This measure is applied in chapter 8 below.

such studies must include, as explicit variables, the preferences of the people and of their rival claimants for power.

Quasi-ideological debates about community and national power structures can be interpreted as conflicting hypotheses about the size of coefficients in a simple indirect influence structure. In figure 7.2, U_1 represents the preferences of a putative elite (e.g., Social and Economic Notables of New Haven; or, on the national level, members of the Council on Foreign Relations). U_2 indicates the preferences of the people or voters. U_3 denotes the preferences of government officials, or, more typically, some subset of officialdom (most often, in our era, members of the executive branch). Y_4 represents the outcome variable.

Among the competing theories that the diagram helps specify are the following:

Elective Oligarchy. In pure form, this hypothesis holds that d_{43} is large, while all other coefficients are insignificant. Proponents of this position, usually liberals disillusioned by the *Pentagon Papers*, Watergate, and similar revelations, hold that the executive branch (or in a nonelective variant, the military) is "out of control"; that is, no longer subject to popular influence (d_{32} is low or zero). The possibility of indirect elite domination (a significant d_{31}) is usually dismissed or ignored by such observers, who remain hopeful that conventional politics can restore democracy.

Ruling Elite. Theories of this type hold that both d_{43} and d_{31} are substantial, while (in traditional versions) d_{32} is thought to be low. The most famous example is, of course, the Marxist view that the government is merely the executive committee of the ruling class; but non-Marxists such as Domhoff (1967) and Barnet (1971) present evidence about the background of U.S. government elites that supports a theory of this type, at least with respect to foreign policy.

Popular Control. The democratic hypothesis, obviously, is that d_{32} and d_{43} are large, while d_{31} and d_{21} are insignificant, or at least small. One statistical study on the national level,

that of Miller and Stokes (1963), attempted to test this hypothesis with respect to congressional votes. They found significant popular (constituency) control over civil rights issues,
lower control over social welfare votes, and no control over
foreign policy decisions. Their study did not, however, test
the effect of possible elites. On the local level, Dahl (1961)
attempted to gauge both elite and mass influence. After
establishing the d_{43} link, he inferred the absence of elite
influence from the fact that its members did not initiate
policy, and then attributed substantial control over officials
to the people, on the basis of evidence suggesting anticipation
of electoral reactions.

Manipulative Elite Rule. The final hypothesis is frequently
the fall-back position of those who favor elite theories when
evidence suggests that d_{32} is large. This view, best known
through the writings of Marcuse (1964) and also suggested
by Bachrach and Baratz (1962), holds that d_{21} is large. Thus
the elite ultimately controls even if popular preferences seem
to prevail.

One advantage of the path analysis framework is that it
poses the choice among theories in quantitative rather than
qualitative terms. It is perfectly possible that both d_{31} and
d_{32} will be significant, and that d_{21} will be large, but less than
one. The question thus becomes "how much elite influence?"
instead of an either / or choice between "ruling elite" and
"democracy."

A second advantage of casting power theories in this way is
that it suggests research designs. This is not to say that such
research will be easy. Estimation of coefficients in figure 7.2
would prove nothing unless the causal ordering can be substantiated. Establishing causal precedence among preference
variables is a grave difficulty, especially when influence over
preferences is accomplished quickly or continuously.[3] Time-

3. In such cases, preferences of influencer and influencee are likely not to
   differ, or to differ only slightly, at any moment. Consequently, there will
   be no overt conflict between them. Quick or continuous causation of
   preferences by preferences is one source of "nondecisions" (Bachrach and
   Baratz, 1962).

series data can help determine the direction of causation—for example, if polls show that governmental foreign policy actions lead, rather than follow, popular opinion. More often, writers resort to known (or suspected) mechanisms to substantiate causal attributions. Thus, Leftist publications devote a great deal of attention to processes by which elite organizations mold public and official opinion. Conversely, conventional liberals usually point to elections to justify their belief that the people rule. Statistical causal inference might select between conflicting mechanisms, if alternative overdetermined theories can be specified.

Attenuation and Obsolescence

Although sources of ultimate influence should not be neglected, it is a mistake to carry the regress of power attribution too far, especially through time. Two considerations suggest this conclusion: attenuation of influence and obsolescence of preferences.

Attenuation. Because path coefficients normally do not exceed one, and are likely to be less, the greater the number of links intervening between an ultimate cause and an outcome, the smaller the compound path coefficient measuring the effect of that cause. Eventually, we reach a point of insignificance in both social and explanatory power. Thus there are usually diminishing returns the farther back the search for "ultimate power" extends.

This argument must be qualified when indirect influence operates through several causal chains. Since the total effect is obtained by summing over the chains, even a fairly remote cause can be important if it operates through enough channels.

Obsolescence. When indirect influence takes a long time to accomplish an effect, a second danger arises. The longer the time span between an actor's supposedly causal preference and the final outcome, the greater the probability that the actor will have changed his preference by the time the outcome occurs. Consequently, ambiguity arises in attributing power. If the actor's preference at time $t(1)$, $U(1)$, ultimately affects outcome $Y(m)$ at time $t(m)$, do we want to assign power to him if his current preference $U(m)$ is opposed to $U(1)$?

Suppose that America's fanatic anti-Communism of the Cold War era originally stemmed from the machinations of anxious capitalists during the aftermath of the Russian Revolution. Suppose also (purely hypothetically!) that capitalists are now less anti-Communist than the rest of the population and, as a result, are hindered in their efforts to turn a profit by trading with Communist countries. To attribute such results of anti-Communism as the Vietnam War to the power of capitalists would then be seriously misleading (especially as a guide to action), even if the historical analysis were correct. Of course, if capitalists continue to foster anti-Communism, a different conclusion might be in order.

Perhaps we ought only to conclude from this that power, like steering ability generally, is inversely related to the time lag between action and response. However, because of the possible ambiguity arising from preference obsolescence, power studies (as distinguished from studies of historical causality), should not be carried back too far in time.

Attenuation and obsolescence also point to fallacies in the parlor game of trying to attribute influence over contemporary events to long-dead prophets or emperors. Often it makes no sense to define their preferences for current outcomes. And, if we could estimate the structure by which their influence was transmitted from their time to ours, their attenuated coefficients would be so small that any discernible effect must be attributed more to good luck than to statistically predictable influence.

A related argument applies to the influence of contemporary ideologues, nonconformists, and gadflies. Their statistically predictable influence is generally low, unless they possess power resources. Nevertheless, their effect on some outcomes may be great for one or more of three reasons: (a) good luck; (b) the sheer volume of their expressed preferences, so that even with low influence coefficients, some are likely to have effect; or (*c*) the intensity with which they pursue especially strong preferences, which offsets low coefficients in determining total impact on particular events.

PREFERENCES VS. INTERESTS

Many classic questions of social theory revolve around the distinction between subjective preferences and objective interests. Who is the best judge of a person's interests? Should an elected representative comply with her constituency's desires or adhere to her view of their true interests? Should a government be judged by the conformity of its policies to people's needs or their wants?

In defining power as causation by preferences, I have opted to keep the concept within the empiricist tradition, which bases analysis on subjective wants.[4] To do otherwise, it seems to me, would make "power" more relevant to normative than to empirical analysis, since it is hard to obtain agreement about objective interests. Even accepting this basic position, there remain questions related to the interest-preference distinction which sometimes make the meaning of power ambiguous. The remainder of this chapter points out two such possibilities and attempts to resolve difficulties they pose.

Discrepancy between Preference Reductions[5]

In chapter 3, the concept of preference was described using two conditional definitions. One applies before an outcome (*Y*) happens; the other, after the event. Can the two reductions yield different results? Might an actor choose *Y* before it happens, but react negatively to the experience of *Y*?

4. My analysis is, however, compatible with related concerns of writers who emphasize objective interests. Defining power in terms of preference instead of behavior makes it possible to measure power when there is no behavioral conflict. Similarly, the analysis of indirect power responds to Balbus (1971), who insists that determination of wants either be included in the meaning of power or be studied as an essential adjunct to power analysis.

5. I am indebted to Corty Camann for bringing this problem to my attention.

This is indeed a common phenomenon, and it creates difficulty in power attribution. For example, a father offers his daughter a peach ice cream cone, but the child, never having eaten that flavor, resists. The father insists, confident the girl will enjoy the experience. Sure enough, she is delighted. Should we attribute power to the father, or did he merely anticipate the child's ultimate reaction? The question has obvious political analogues whenever leaders claim to be more farsighted than citizens.

The discrepancy between reductions is related to, but not identical with, the broader distinction of objective interests and subjective wants. It is reasonable to say that trying peach ice cream was in the child's interest because the idea of objective interest seems to imply possibility of conversion to subjective preference, given appropriate conditions such as experience of the outcome (Balbus, 1971:168–72). But not everything desired after experience is in one's interest— heroin, for example.

The question of interest aside, how shall we handle reduction discrepancies in allocating power? One response is to deny the possibility of attributing power, since the defining preference is ambiguous. After all, two conditional definitions of a single concept should give the same result for the same object. But in the case we are considering, the object treated by the two reductions is not the same, for the second reduction requires that the actor have experienced the outcome. Experience can change preferences.

The resolution I advocate gives priority to the preference existing before the outcome. This alternative is more appealing intuitively and more parsimonious theoretically, for the factors determining the result of an overt conflict between two actors are doubtless the same whether or not one actor will change his mind after experiencing the outcome.[6]

6. Less tractable to analysis are persons who consistently act as though they prefer different outcomes before and after events. Bateson et al. (1956) suggest such individuals may induce schizophrenia in others dependent upon them.

Table 7.1. Priorities When the Two Conditional Definitions of Preference Give Conflicting Results

Before Y Occurs	*After Y Occurs*		
	A Prefers Y	A Unaware of Y or Indifferent	A Prefers not-Y
A Prefers Y	R-I and R-II Consistent	R-I Prevails	R-I Prevails
A Unaware of Y or Indifferent	R-II Prevails	R-I and R-II Consistent	R-II Prevails
A Prefers not-Y	R-I Prevails	R-I Prevails	R-I and R-II Consistent

Table 7.1 presents nine possible relations between A's preference before and after the occurrence of Y. The cells of the table show which conditional definition should be followed in power analysis: *R-I*, the reduction based on choice behavior before the outcome, or *R-II*, the reduction based on reactions after the event. In case of a discrepancy, preferences are defined for purposes of power analysis by *R-II* only when A is unaware of Y, or indifferent before the event. In this situation, an alert respondent may anticipate A's reaction and be guided by it, despite A's present inactivity. In all other cases of reduction discrepancy, power should be defined using the preference revealed by *R-I*.

Power and Leadership in Marxist Systems[7]

Marxists typically distinguish between subjective wants, which can reflect false consciousness, and objective interests, usually class-linked (Balbus, 1971). A chief function of the vanguard party is to induce the masses to perceive their true interests; and the purpose of a Communist government, at least in the Maoist version, is to serve the people, to further

7. The analysis that follows can apply also in non-Marxist systems, but the issues relate most directly to Marxist ideas.

the objective interests of the people. It is sometimes said that only such leadership can truly give power to the people—a view strenuously opposed by liberal democrats (e.g., Sartori, 1962).

The purpose of this subsection is to depict the ideal role of Communist leadership using a simplified causal structure. This enables us to treat several possibilities recognized by Marxists in the same terms as our general power analysis. In the process, we find one case where the idea of indirect power is debatable. The following discussion relies on figure 7.3.

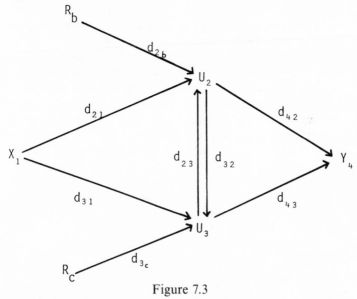

Figure 7.3

In the diagram, X_1 denotes the objective interests of the masses. No claim is made that agreement can be reached on this variable, but we shall assume it exists.[8] U_2 represents the

8. One approach to the concept of objective interest might be through the analysis of rationality in collective action, as advanced by Olson (1965) and Hardin (1971), among others. Braybrooke (1969) suggests another line of attack with his notion of a welfare census.

policy preferences of party leadership. U_3 indicates the subjective policy preferences of the masses. Y_4, the outcome variable, might represent government policies in a Communist system, or revolutionary actions when the party operates within a capitalist or feudal system.

If the party first comes into contact with the masses in a bourgeois democracy, the prevailing causal relation may be the path $d_{3c}d_{43}$, as an elite manipulates the people into false consciousness. The purpose of the party, whether in a pre- or post-revolutionary situation, is to shape its own preferences according to the interests of the masses (d_{21}), then to influence the masses to adopt those policies (d_{32}) and to aid the masses to put them into effect (d_{43}). In this effort, the party must avoid several pitfalls. Through isolation from the people or selfishness, it may allow its preferences to be shaped primarily by factors other than the interests of the people $(d_{2b}$ predominates over $d_{21})$.[9] Excessive eagerness for premature popularity may induce it to pander to false consciousness $(d_{3c}d_{23}$ is large). Or, impatience may cause cadres to fall into the errors of elitism or commandism, the attempt to put policies into effect directly (d_{42}), without first changing the desires of the people (d_{32}) and then working through them (d_{43}).

The power interpretation of most paths in the diagram is clear-cut. The direct and indirect power of the people, however misguided, is indicated by the compound path coefficient

9. According to Mao (1943), coincidence of cadres' policy and popular interests is guaranteed by following the dictum "from the masses, to the masses." This means: "take the ideas of the masses (scattered and unsystematic ideas) and concentrate them (through study turn them into concentrated and systematic ideas), then go to the masses and propagate and explain these ideas until the masses embrace them as their own, hold fast to them and translate them into action, and test the correctness of these ideas in such action. Then once again concentrate ideas from the masses and once again go to the masses so that the ideas are persevered in and carried through. And so on, over and over again in an endless spiral, with the ideas becoming more correct, more vital and richer each time." This dynamic, interactive, and iterative process is very inadequately depicted by the simple model in figure 7.3, even with the reciprocal link between U_2 and U_3.

sum $(d_{31}d_{43} + d_{3C}d_{43} + d_{31}d_{23}d_{42} + d_{3C}d_{23}d_{42})$. The power of the cadres is measured by $(d_{2b}d_{42} + d_{2b}d_{32}d_{43} + d_{21}d_{42})$.

The path $d_{21}d_{32}d_{43}$, however, seems less surely interpreted in power terms. Its analogue in figure 7.2, which we used to depict possible U.S. power structures, is the path from elite preferences through popular preferences to policy outcomes. This we interpreted as indirect elite power. Should we interpret the path presently in question differently merely because preferences of this elite are shaped by objective interests of the people? I suspect that many who admit that people have objective interests might wish to do so, perhaps by saying that the magnitude of the path reflects the power of the people, as aided by socialist leadership and correct analysis.

The question is perhaps semantic, as most people would evaluate any elite more highly if it works through the masses in the interests of the masses. Does it matter whether we say the process indicates the power of the people or of the leaders? The semantic decision may nevertheless have practical effects—for example, in the extent of democracy we perceive in the People's Republic of China.

8   EMPIRICAL POWER MEASUREMENT

The abstract quality of the preceding chapters may leave the reader uncertain about how to apply the methods suggested there or even doubtful that they have any practical value. Consequently, in this chapter I discuss key decisions researchers must make in order to use the proposed measures. Then I demonstrate path analytic power measurement and inference with data drawn from Miller and Stokes (1963), whose pioneering study of constituency influence on Congress shows that power *can* be assessed in the way I advocate.[1]

REQUISITE DECISIONS

A theme of this book is that descriptive power analysis should be governed by the same methods as other causal research. Consequently, there is no point in trying to duplicate the advice of expert methodologists. Instead, I comment briefly on certain issues only to offer power analysts a starting point and to apply my perspective to controversies in the power literature.[2]

1. More recent inspiration is provided by Jackson's (1971) paper on "Statistical Models of Senate Roll Call Voting." Neither Jackson nor Miller and Stokes advocate a general conception of power or influence, but their papers treat preferences as independent variables in explaining significant political outcomes, freely referring to the relations detected as "influence." Neither work utilizes path analysis per se, but each estimates coefficients using closely related methods. Although flaws are present in both papers, their importance lies in the demonstration that research of this type can be usefully undertaken.

   Research of related interest by Davis, Dempster, and Wildavsky (1966) is also methodologically instructive. They performed regression analyses of time-series data relating congressional budgetary appropriations and agency budget requests.

2. The suggestions that follow might be compared with earlier proposals on how to study power—e.g., Dahl (1958), Polsby (1963), Bachrach and Baratz (1962, 1963), Payne (1968), Gitlin (1965), McFarland (1969), and Frey (1971).

Selection of Outcome Categories

Since statements about causation, and therefore power, are meaningless without a dependent variable, the first step in any power study must be to answer the question "Power over *what*?" This requires specification of scope, domain, and time period: congressional civil-rights votes during 1959–1960 (Miller and Stokes), all roll-call votes of Senator Hruska during 1960–1961 (Jackson, 1971), New Haven redevelopment decisions from 1950 to 1959 (Dahl, 1961). In selecting outcomes to study, power researchers must often confront three issues: (*a*) breadth of outcome categories, (*b*) "importance," and (*c*) "nondecisions."[3]

Breadth of Outcome Categories. Outcome categories should be broad enough to permit sufficient observations for statistical analysis, yet narrow enough that influence processes can be assumed reasonably constant over the entire set. If there is doubt about this assumption, the data should be reanalyzed to see whether coefficients are similar when the outcome category is divided into subcategories.[4] Division may be by scope (Miller and Stokes found different influence relations for civil rights, foreign policy, and social welfare issues), by domain (the majority leader may influence Democrats but not Republicans), by time period (as at the "shift points" detected by Davis et al., 1966), or by a combination of these three.

Testing the constant process assumption is important for two reasons—one scientific; the other, both scientific and ideological. First, if categories actually subject to different

---

3. On the latter two topics, see especially Frey (1971).
4. An interesting conflict exists between the results of Miller and Stokes, who find different influence coefficients for three issue-areas, and Jackson, who argues that a constant-process model best fits his data. Jackson's test of the constant-process assumption is inadequate, however, because he uses a much cruder model when subdividing by scope. Unless compelling reasons exist for doing otherwise, the same model should be employed for both the grand category and the subdivided categories. The test is to see whether *coefficients* change between subcategories.

influence processes are grouped together in a single model, the explanatory power of that model will be low. Second, the constancy of influence over different scopes is a main point of contention between pluralists and elitists. As the pluralists correctly argue, it must be established by empirical test.

Importance. In an excellent article, Frey (1971) questions the wisdom of seeking to select outcomes for study on the basis of "importance," however defined. Correctly perceiving that the implicit goal of this search "is generalizing to '*the* power structure' of the unit," he urges researchers instead to choose issues according to their intrinsic interest and to avoid "the notion of '*the* power structure' of a social unit [as] a dangerously misleading siren." Generalizations should be based upon the degree of correspondence among power structures for the various distinguishable issues.

As a scientific strategy, Frey's argument has great merit, and I sympathize with it. Nevertheless, the value-laden problem of importance is unlikely to vanish, even if power analysts can restrain the impulse to generalize and simplify. The reader with limited time must decide which outcomes are most worth learning about. The choice does not depend entirely on personal values. To the extent that some outcomes causally determine others, they are objectively more important. In power analysis, several types of outcomes having such priority are especially worthy of study: (*a*) those which affect the preferences of actors controlling other outcomes; (*b*) those which affect power structures governing other outcomes; and (*c*) those which determine whether other outcomes can occur at all. For a more extensive discussion, including formal tests for these and other importance criteria, see Nagel (1972: ch. 10).

Nondecisions. In a major contribution, Bachrach and Baratz (1962, 1963) pointed out that outcomes over which power is exercised include "nondecisions"—potentially significant issues which never reach the agenda of political controversy.[5] The methods I advocate are compatible with measurement of power over nondecisions. In this they differ from the decision-making method of Dahl and other pluralists, which restricts power research to overtly contested issues. Nondecisions are outcomes just as decisions are. Preferences for nondecision outcomes can be measured, and causal analyses can relate those preferences and outcomes.

The (non-) establishment of socialism in the United States is a highly significant nonissue over which influence might be measured. A set of proposals drawn from the programs of socialist parties here and abroad could constitute the outcome category (e.g., nationalization of various industries, workers' participation in management, national health insurance, redistribution of income and assets, etc.). Over each nonevent in the outcome category, preferences might be measured for different actors. If workers favor most of the proposals, and stockholders oppose them, one might infer that failure to establish socialism in the U.S. is due to the influence of the propertied classes. The conclusion would be more firmly established, of course, if one could demonstrate *how* stockholders exercised influence over the outcome.[6]

If both groups oppose socialist policies, influence might explain the outcome only trivially—the system performs as the vast majority desire. If, however, data could be produced to demonstrate a causal relation between owners' and workers' preferences, the influence hypothesis might be restored in more complex form.[7]

5. See also the valuable discussion in McFarland (1969 : ch. 5).
6. Confidence in a causal ordering rises when the "density" (Samuelson, 1965) of the analysis is increased by including intervening variables. Frey (1971) insists on this point.
7. See Bachrach and Baratz on mobilization of bias, information manipulation, and reinforcement of existing values and attitudes. See also Nagel (1968) for a way to conceptualize such influence mathematically. Statistical causal analyses of continuous attitude reinforcement might be extraordinarily difficult, but efforts to reinforce are certainly observable, even if proof of their effect is not easy.

Construction of Models

Although analysts may be tempted to devise models for estimation and testing *after* gathering data, it is imperative to do so *before* final field research. Experimentalists cannot escape this principle; but it applies equally to those who depend on cross-sectional or time-series data. Tests among conflicting causal orderings may depend upon time-series data, which the investigator may fail to collect unless she anticipates the need for such tests. Similarly, to estimate a nonrecursive model may require additional ("instrumental") variables. If the model is proposed after data are collected, it will be too late to make the necessary observations.[8]

Two other aspects of model-specification merit extended comment: the necessity of testing alternative models and the selection of actors.

Necessity of Alternatives.[9] Path coefficient estimates are entirely relative to the causal model employed in analyzing the data; and more than one model can fit the same data, by satisfying test equations. Therefore, power measures obtained by estimating a single model can be practically worthless. Consequently, it is essential to seek every reasonable alternative model that might explain an outcome. Since a lone researcher's sensitivity to alternatives may be dulled by his own theoretical or ideological tendencies, it is wise to seek hypotheses from theorists of opposed viewpoints.

Some proffered hypotheses can be rejected a priori, as inconsistent with previous evidence or general principles of causal specification, or as impossible to estimate. Studies that conscientiously test all remaining possibilities have three advantages over those restricted to solitary models: (*a*) If the single theory fails to fit the data, the investigator has only

8. Stokes (1971), reflecting on lessons of his own study with Miller, comments, "Elegant reanalysis is a poor remedy for opportunities missed at the stage of design."

9. For comments on power researchers' failure to state alternative models, see Dahl (1968).

reduced the universe of possibilities by one. A multiple-hypothesis study is more likely to reveal one or more theories that do fit. Future work can build on these unrejected models. (*b*) If the single hypothesis does fit the data, researcher or readers may jump to the conclusion that it truly measures power over the outcome. In a multiple-model study, other unrejected structures may appear, forcing more judicious interpretation. (*c*) Critics of a single-model study can always argue that their own favorite explanations have not yet been disproved. Research that tests alternatives may forestall such arguments.

Since statistical tests alone do not always decide between conflicting specifications, power researchers should not only gather data on preferences and outcomes, but should also undertake other observations that aid in detecting causal mechanisms.[10] Case studies of decisions, interviews with participants, examination of structural factors promoting indirect influence, and inferences from general theory all play a role in determining the existence and / or direction of influence.

Selection of Actors. By definition, any model of influence must include preferences of actors as variables causally prior to the outcome. What types of actors should appear?

1. The power of individuals is generally of transitory interest. The significant questions about power concern its distribution among social aggregates and institutional categories—economic classes, interest groups, organizations, hierarchical levels, organizational roles, ideological factions. As Wrong (1968 : 680) rightly says, "The study of power relations among groups is a more important task for political sociology than the identification of powerful individuals." The preferences of collective entities offer an additional advantage in that they are likely to be more enduring and better-suited to statistical analysis.

2. Often two or more actors exercise little or no power separately, but are able to affect outcomes whenever they

10. I am indebted to Bill Panning for suggesting this point. See also Frey (1971).

agree sufficiently to act in concert. In such cases, it is necessary to measure the power of the coalition in addition to, or instead of, the power of its individual members. If the members agree almost perfectly concerning all outcomes within a category, they should be treated as a single actor.[11] If they agree less often, but are thought to be more effective when in accord, a term representing the product of their preferences should be added to the model.[12] The coefficient for this term will measure the power of the coalition.

3. Contrary to Lasswell and Kaplan's definition of power as "participation in the making of decisions," it is *not* necessary that an actor participate, overtly or covertly, in decisions about an outcome in order to have power over it. Anticipated reactions, information manipulation, provision of resources to surrogates, and mobilization of bias amply justify including preferences of nonparticipants as causal influences.

Operationalization of Variables

The indispensable variables in any descriptive power study are outcomes and preferences.

Outcomes. Four steps are necessary to establish an outcome variable: (1) selection of events to observe; (2) determination of the possible states of each event; (3) choice of a measure on the possible states; and (4) observation of which possible state actually occurs.

1. As Frey (1971) notes, selecting events within the outcome category presents difficulties parallel to those faced in selecting the category itself. In particular, two essentially unsolvable problems pose difficult choices for the researcher and offer ammunition to critics of almost any power study.

First, the outcome variable can be construed to include "nonevents" as well as visible happenings. Whether or not to do so depends partly on the outcome category. The category "Senate roll-call votes" (Jackson, 1971) excludes nonevents

11. See the discussion of multicollinearity in chapter 10.
12. Cf. equations 5.24 and 5.25 above.

by definition. A broader category (e.g., racial policy during the 1950s) might permit or even demand inclusion of non-events (potential civil rights legislation that never reached a vote due to fear of a Southern filibuster).

Second, unless equal "importance" is guaranteed by the selection criterion, weighting of outcomes according to importance may be desirable.[13] In assessing power over votes of the New Haven Board of Aldermen, it is absurd to count a multimillion dollar redevelopment appropriation equally with the "petition of the Morris Cove 59 Groaners for an appropriation of $500 to help defray expenses of their annual Easter Egg Hunt and Halloween Parade."[14]

2. After the fact, any event has a definite character, but this consists only in the occurrence of one among two or more possibilities. A bill that passed could have failed; an appropriation of three million dollars might have taken any value from zero on up; a conflict ending in the total victory of one side might have ended in its defeat, or in a variety of compromises. A listing of the *possible states* of each event is an essential prerequisite to measuring both outcomes and preferences. The possible states of an event may take the form of a set with two or more members, or of a continuum, either closed or open-ended.

3. The outcome measure is a function defined on the possible states of the events. Measures at any level are possible—nominal (assignment of 1 to a bill that passes, 0 to a bill that fails); ordinal (numerical ranking of policies from least to most liberal); interval (attitude toward Communism);[15] or ratio (dollars appropriated, hours worked). As I noted in chapter 5, however, the validity of path analysis for ordinal scales is subject to debate.

13. This is especially so when binary preference measures are used. Ordinal and interval preferences at least offer the possibility of weighting according to actors' subjective feeling of relative importance (relative priority or intensity of concern).
14. New Haven *Aldermanic Journal*, March 2, 1970, p. 123.
15. See Upshaw (1968) for attitude scaling techniques that yield interval measures.

4. Observability of outcomes can range from routinely easy (roll-call votes) to virtually impossible (domestic policy decisions in a totally closed society). Since the outcome concept is so general, methods for observing outcomes are coextensive with the entire array of social science observation techniques; and so there is no point in elaborating on the topic here.

Preferences. Measurement and observation of preferences will be a fundamental difficulty in the study of power, severely restricting outcomes over which power can be measured. The preference problem is hardly unique to influence analysis, however, for the concept is also basic to motivation theory in psychology (Irwin, 1958), conflict theory (Axelrod, 1970), game theory, decision theory, and microeconomics. Here, as in pointing to the use of standard statistical methods, my conception of power unites the study of influence with the mainstream of social science methodology and theory.

The preference measure, like the outcome measure, is a function defined on the possible states of each outcome event. A separate measure is required for each actor.

All preference measures must at least order possible outcome states. The simplest two-valued ordering (approve–disapprove, 1–0) is suited, like other dichotomous variables, to analysis using path algorithms. In the absence of a proof of path algorithms for other ordinal variables, the availability of interval preference measures becomes a potentially important question in power research. In economics, the debate between proponents of ordinal and cardinal utility (i.e., ordinal and interval or ratio preference measures) has produced a vast formal literature and even a few empirical studies.[16] The best-known cardinal utility, that of Von Neumann and Morgenstern, is probably not practical for large-scale field studies.[17] Fortunately, psychologists have

16. For reviews, see Luce and Raiffa (1957: ch. 2) and Luce and Suppes (1965).
17. Its axioms are given in Luce and Raiffa (1957: 23–32). Researchers who do employ the Von Neumann–Morgenstern utility should be aware of an additional danger. The most obvious way to obtain the utilities would

invented attitude scales that produce interval measures.[18] In addition, as I have noted, some experts argue that ordinal scales can be analyzed using interval-level procedures (Tufte, 1969). Both Jackson and Miller and Stokes use interval-level analysis on ordinal (Guttman) scales.

Whatever the level of measurement attained or assumed, the investigator must be aware that numerical measures of power could differ, perhaps dramatically, if a different level were employed. Consider two actors whose preference intensities covary over outcome events, though they always prefer different possibilities. Suppose one actor gets her way on events about which both care little, while the second actor prevails on the less frequent occasions when both have intense preferences. Dichotomous (approve–disapprove, win–lose) measures would assign greater power to the first actor; interval measures might give it to the second, an intuitively more satisfactory result. In general, the higher the level of measurement of both preferences and outcomes, the better the power measures.

Because preferences are dispositions, observing them poses problems not encountered in observing events. Strictly speaking, preferences should be observed by noting behavior under conditions specified in one or more reduction sentences for the concept, such as the two in chapter 3. Unfortunately, such conditions may be hard to satisfy outside the laboratory. Consequently, a variety of substitute strategies may be employed. A partial listing follows.[19]

---

be by offering lottery choices involving the most preferred possible state of each outcome *event*. The result will be preference measures ranging from zero to one over the possible states of each event. Consequently, the measure will not distinguish differing intensities of preference from event to event. This pitfall might be avoided by offering lotteries involving the single most preferred possible state drawn from all the possible states of all the events within the outcome category—if actors are able to make the required discriminations.

18. See Upshaw (1968).
19. These suggestions are largely compiled from Duncan (1969), Axelrod (1970), and Upshaw (1968).

1. Interviewing techniques include (*a*) direct questions ("Do you prefer *A* or *B*?" "Assign a number from 1 to 100 to each alternative, indicating how strongly you desire it."), (*b*) indirect questions (as in a Thurstone scale), and (*c*) offers of hypothetical choices (usually a necessity to obtain Von Neumann–Morgenstern utilities).

2. Inferences can be drawn from assumed or known causes and correlates of preferences. Experimental psychologists assume a rat deprived of water is intensely rewarded by it; so might the investigator of preferences assume (but not without risk!) that a poor person values ten dollars more than a millionaire. In laboratory games, it is taken for granted that participants prefer larger payoff quantities of pennies or points; similarly, it might be assumed that participants in real "games" monotonically prefer larger quantities of their payoffs—capitalists, profits; politicians, votes; bureaucrats, appropriations. Hazards of this strategy are obvious; but with advances in the psychology and sociology of motivation, it may eventually be utilized with greater confidence.

3. Inferences about preferences can also be made from their assumed or known behavioral consequences. Content analysis falls in this category. In a study of power within a British corporation, Pettigrew (1972) inferred a manager's preference from an analysis of his correspondence. Other persistent patterns of both choice behavior and expressive behavior may reveal preferences.

Addenda

Two additional aspects of data gathering in power studies deserve brief comment: (*a*) preferences of collective actors; and (*b*) temporal relations between preference and outcome observations.

Group Preferences. Despite traditional aversions to "group minds," observation of collective preferences seems to me to offer few unusual difficulties, other than hard work and expense.

When the collective actor is an unorganized aggregate, its preference can be inferred by, among other methods, observing preferences of a sample of members and from them developing a composite index. Miller and Stokes do this in measuring constituency preferences. If sample variance is extremely high, however, it may make no sense to treat the collectivity as an actor having a distinguishable preference. When high variance results from a multi-modal distribution, the problem might be solved by dividing the collectivity into two or more group actors.

Organized collectivities, such as nations, labor unions, and corporations, usually have formally designated decision-making roles. Behavior and statements of their incumbents can be used in inferring preferences, using techniques of the types described above.

Time Sequences. Unfortunately, most power studies are likely to use cross-sectional data, precluding time sequence as a basis for causal ordering. This problem has, however, been addressed by Duncan (1969), who uses path analysis to show implications of differing causal orderings when dispositions are hypothetical causes and their indices are observed at the same time as dependent variables. Nevertheless, it is obvious that time-series data are highly desirable, especially when preferences themselves are thought to be causally ordered, as in models of indirect influence.

PATH ANALYSIS OF CONSTITUENCY INFLUENCE ON CONGRESS[20]

This section illustrates the use of empirical data in a path analysis of political influence. The results demonstrate the potential inconclusiveness of path analytic causal inference, as two models are compatible with the data. Nevertheless, four plausible theories are eliminated, one on the basis of time sequences, one by theory trimming, and two by test equations.

20. I am indebted to Vincent McHale, who first suggested the relevance of this literature to my ideas on power.

The two unrejected models show a high degree of substantive agreement.

Estimation and Evaluation of Six Models

The data employed are taken from Miller and Stokes (1963). They used four variables to analyze the influence of constituencies on their representatives' votes: the average attitude of constituents in a district (U_1); the representative's perception of his constituency's attitude (X_2); the representative's own policy attitudes (U_3); and the representative's roll-call voting behavior (Y_4). Each variable was measured for a sample of congresspersons and their districts; measures of the first three factors were obtained in 1958 from questionnaires. Three issue-areas were studied, but the authors provide a detailed analysis for civil rights only. Table 8.1 presents simple correlations among the variables in that area.[21]

Table 8.1. Correlations among Variables Pertaining to Civil Rights

	X_2	U_3	Y_4
U_1	.738	.498	.649
X_2	–	.643	.823
U_3	–	–	.721

As I noted in chapter 6, four variables can generate 4096 models. Many can be dismissed a priori. All models that propose the representative's votes, private beliefs, or perceptions cause the constituency's attitude seem dubious. Elimination of such models leaves only 512 in contention! Only six are examined below; all but the first have appeared previously in the literature.

Model I. Model I is a straightforward power comparison. Two actors, representative and constituency, are viewed as competing for influence over a single outcome, the representative's votes. Which has greater influence? Or, in different

21. These correlations are not those originally used by Miller and Stokes (1963). Instead, they are coefficients corrected for attenuation, as reported by Cnudde and McCrone (1966).

terms, does the representative vote according to the dictates of her conscience or according to the wishes of the people who elected her? The causal effect of constituency preferences is mediated by the congressperson's (imperfect) perception of those preferences; and the correlation between the preferences of constituency and representative must be taken into account, although it is given no causal interpretation (figure 8.1).[22]

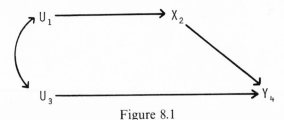

Figure 8.1

Using the path algorithms developed in chapter 5 estimation equations may be written by inspection. These equations allow one to solve quickly for the path coefficients in terms of known correlations.

Estimation Equations

$$r_{12} = d_{21} = .738 \tag{8.1a}$$

$$r_{24} = d_{42} + d_{21}r_{13}d_{43} = .823 \tag{8.1b}$$

$$r_{34} = r_{13}d_{21}d_{42} + d_{43} = .721 \tag{8.1c}$$

The last two equations can be solved simultaneously to yield:[23]

$$d_{42} = .645$$

$$d_{43} = .484$$

The measure of the representative's "own" influence over her votes is then $d_{43} = .484$, while the constituency's influence

22. Residuals are omitted to simplify the diagram.
23. All computations are to slide-rule accuracy only.

is given by the compound coefficient $d_{421} = d_{42}d_{21} = (.645)$ $(.738) = .476$. Model I implies, then, that the two actors have nearly equal influence, with a slight, but probably insignificant edge to the representative.

These power "measures" are, however, only as good as the model from which they are derived. If the model is incorrect, the measures are worthless. Fortunately, Model I is over-identified, two links having been specified zero a priori. Therefore, it is possible to judge its validity by using the equations for r_{23} and r_{14} as test equations:

$$r_{14} = d_{21}d_{42} + r_{13}d_{43} \qquad (8.2a)$$

$$r_{23} = d_{21}r_{13} \qquad (8.2b)$$

The actual value of r_{14} is .649. When path coefficient estimates derived from Model I are substituted into equation 8.2a, the result is .717, a discrepancy of .068. The second test equation yields a more serious difference. The actual value of r_{23} is .643, but the value predicted by the model is only .368, a difference of .275.

Model I therefore should be rejected, along with the measures derived from it. This conclusion illustrates both the dependence of power measures on a theoretical model, and the utility of path analytic causal inference, which enables us to reject a plausible, if simplistic, model.

Model II. Model II and all subsequent models are not simple influence-comparison models. Instead, they assume the system contains only one "unmoved mover"—the constituency, whose attitudes are assumed to affect, directly or indirectly, the personal preferences of the representative.[24] The focus of interest, as in the original Miller–Stokes study, is upon the way in which the presumed constituency influence operates. Does the constituency exert influence by favoring candidates whose general policy preferences correspond to its own? Does the representative, regardless of his personal beliefs,

24. Nevertheless, power comparisons remain possible and will be made later in the chapter.

adjust his behavior to his perception of the constituency's position? Or does the truth rest in some complex mixture of these two modes of influence?

Model II, in simple-minded fashion, tests between the first two alternatives by including one path for each (figure 8.2).[25]

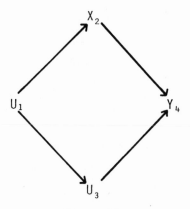

Figure 8.2

Model II differs from Model I only in the causal interpretation given the U_1–U_3 link. Coefficient estimates are identical, except for the addition of d_{31}, which equals r_{13}.

If Model II were valid, the influence exercised via the representative's perception and via his own beliefs would be measured, respectively, by $d_{21}d_{42} = .476$, and $d_{31}d_{43} = .241$. One might incautiously conclude that constituencies control their representatives much less by candidate selection than by the congresspersons' yielding to constituents' perceived preferences. Once again, however, the model itself must be evaluated. Test equation results are also identical to those for Model I. Therefore, Model II must be rejected. The discrepancy

25. Model II is Cnudde and McCrone's Model I. Instead of computing path coefficients, they used the Simon–Blalock procedure to test the model, and obtained the same (negative) results yielded by my test equations.

between actual and predicted values of r_{23} suggests there is some additional link between X_2 and U_3.

Model III.[26] One possibility is a causal link from X_2 to U_3; that is, the representative's own attitudes are influenced by the attitudes she perceives in her constituents. This proposal has both intuitive and psychological plausibility: The malleable politician actually comes to believe that which it is expedient for her to believe; principle adjusts to interest; attitudes are shaped by reward and punishment (figure 8.3).

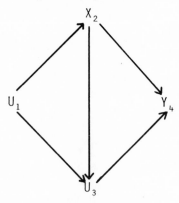

Figure 8.3

Estimation Equations

$r_{12} = d_{21} =$	.738	(8.4a)
$r_{13} = d_{21}d_{32} + d_{31} =$	.498	(8.4b)
$r_{23} = d_{32} + d_{31}d_{21} =$	.643	(8.4c)
$r_{24} = d_{42} + d_{32}d_{43} + d_{21}d_{31}d_{43} =$	.823	(8.4d)
$r_{34} = d_{32}d_{42} + d_{43} + d_{21}d_{31}d_{42} =$	.721	(8.4e)

Solution

$$d_{21} = .738$$
$$d_{31} = .055$$
$$d_{32} = .600$$
$$d_{42} = .611$$
$$d_{43} = .332$$

26. Model III is Miller and Stokes' Model II.

Test Equation	Actual Value	Predicted Value	Difference
$r_{14} = d_{21}d_{42} + d_{21}d_{32}d_{43}$			
$+ d_{31}d_{43}$	.649	.616	.033

Model III fits its test equation closely. However, figure 8.3 is not a proper portrait of the results obtained. One depicted link, that between U_1 and U_3, is so small ($d_{31} = .055$) that it might reasonably be trimmed from the model. The result is Model IIIA, in which it is assumed that constituents' attitudes do not directly affect representatives' beliefs (i.e., the candidate selection link is inoperative).

Model IIIA.[27] According to Heise (1969), the test of whether a path should be trimmed is the ability of the trimmed model to reproduce the correlation matrix.[28] Accordingly, let us compute new coefficients and estimate the test equations for Model IIIA (figure 8.4).[29]

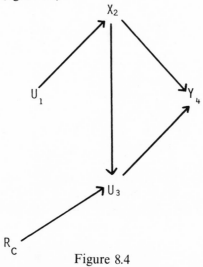

Figure 8.4

27. Model IIIA is Cnudde and McCrone's Model III.
28. But see chapter 5, footnote 32, above.
29. The residual R_c, and its path coefficient, d_{3c}, are included in this and subsequent models because the coefficient is used in the last section.

Estimation Equations

$$r_{12} = d_{21} = \qquad .738 \qquad (8.5a)$$
$$r_{23} = d_{32} = \qquad .643 \qquad (8.5b)$$
$$r_{24} = d_{42} + d_{32}d_{43} = \qquad .823 \qquad (8.5c)$$
$$r_{43} = d_{32}d_{42} + d_{43} = \qquad .721 \qquad (8.5d)$$
$$d_{3c} = \sqrt{1 - d_{21}^2 d_{32}^2} \qquad (8.5e)$$

Solution

$$d_{21} = .738$$
$$d_{32} = .643$$
$$d_{42} = .611$$
$$d_{43} = .329$$
$$d_{3c} = .881$$

Test Equations	Actual Values	Predicted Values	Difference
$r_{13} = d_{21}d_{32}$	.498	.475	.023
$r_{14} = d_{21}d_{42} + d_{21}d_{32}d_{43}$	.649	.607	.042

Since discrepancies between actual and predicted values are slight, Model IIIA may be considered preferable to the less parsimonious Model III.[30]

Model IV. Elimination of the path from U_1 to U_3 is valid only if one accepts all the other causal assumptions built into Model III. If any are changed, the value of d_{31} obtained may be far from zero. This is demonstrated by Model IV (figure 8.5), which modifies only one assumption of Model III. In Model IV the representative's perceptions adjust to his attitudes, instead of the reverse; the congressperson sees what he wants to see. As so often happens in social science, both intuition and psychology make this hypothesis just as plausible as its direct opposite.[31]

30. Less casual tests for significance cannot be undertaken without more data than Miller and Stokes supply.
31. Model IV is the other model evaluated by Miller and Stokes. Forbes and Tufte (1968a) also propose it as an alternative to the theory favored by Cnudde and McCrone (Model IIIA).

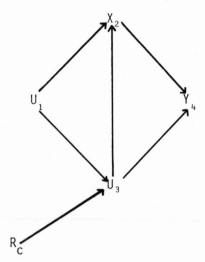

Figure 8.5

Estimation Equations

$$r_{13} = d_{31} = \qquad\qquad .498 \qquad (8.6a)$$
$$r_{12} = d_{21} + d_{31}d_{23} = \qquad\qquad .738 \qquad (8.6b)$$
$$r_{23} = d_{21}d_{31} + d_{23} = \qquad\qquad .643 \qquad (8.6c)$$
$$r_{24} = d_{42} + d_{23}d_{43} + d_{21}d_{31}d_{43} = \qquad .823 \qquad (8.6d)$$
$$r_{34} = d_{23}d_{42} + d_{43} + d_{21}d_{31}d_{42} = \qquad .721 \qquad (8.6e)$$
$$d_{3c} = \sqrt{1 - d_{31}{}^2} \qquad\qquad\qquad (8.6f)$$

Solution

$$d_{21} = .555$$
$$d_{31} = .498$$
$$d_{23} = .367$$
$$d_{42} = .613$$
$$d_{43} = .326$$
$$d_{3c} = .868$$

Test Equation	Actual Value	Predicted Value	Difference
$r_{14} = d_{21}d_{42} + d_{31}d_{23}d_{42}$ $+ d_{31}d_{43}$	.649	.614	.035

Model IV fits the data just as well as Models III and IIIA, despite their conflicting substantive assumptions regarding the X_2–U_3 link.

Model V. Forbes and Tufte (1968a) have shown that a strikingly different theory is numerically compatible with the evidence (figure 8.6).

$$U_1 \longrightarrow X_2 \longrightarrow Y_4 \longrightarrow U_3$$

Figure 8.6

In this causal chain, the congressperson's preferences are assumed not to cause but to result from his voting behavior. This paradoxical premise is a straightforward application of the forced-compliance paradigm of cognitive dissonance theory (Festinger and Carlsmith, 1959), which has been substantiated by experimental evidence. The model proposes that the representative conforms to constituents' perceived preferences, and then rationalizes his lack of independence by adjusting his beliefs to make them consonant with his behavior.

Path estimation of chain models is a trivial exercise:

Estimation Equations

$$r_{12} = d_{21} = .738 \tag{8.7a}$$
$$r_{24} = d_{42} = .823 \tag{8.7b}$$
$$r_{34} = d_{34} = .721 \tag{8.7c}$$

Three test equations are available for this sparsely connected model:

Test Equations	Actual Values	Predicted Values	Difference
$r_{14} = d_{21}d_{42}$	.649	.608	.041
$r_{13} = d_{21}d_{42}d_{34}$	.498	.438	.060
$r_{23} = d_{42}d_{34}$	.643	.594	.049

Since models that include fewer links are less likely to satisfy test equations, one might hesitate before rejecting Model V in favor of Models IIIA or IV on the basis of its slightly inferior fit alone. However, there is an a priori reason for rejecting this model (a possibility which Forbes and Tufte neglect). Preference and perception data were gathered immediately after the 1958 elections, while voting measures are presumably from the following congressional term.[32] Therefore, the principle of temporal sequence suffices to reject Model V.[33]

Nonrecursive Models. All six theories evaluated in the preceding pages are recursive—they contain no two-way causal paths and no loops. There exist many logically possible nonrecursive models containing the four variables, and plausible arguments can be made for some of them. Indeed, the model originally proposed by Miller and Stokes is nonrecursive. It recognizes the possibility of two-way interaction between the representative's private beliefs (U_3) and her perceptions of constituents' attitudes (X_2) (figure 8.7).

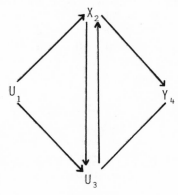

Figure 8.7

32. Miller and Stokes are not explicit about this, but no other possibility makes sense.
33. Veteran representatives, of course, may have adjusted their attitudes to conform to their behavior in *previous* sessions.

Unfortunately, the coefficients of this model are not identifiable. This does not mean that the model can be eliminated from consideration, for identifiability might be achieved by appropriate inclusion of additional variables.[34]

Comments on Methods in Three Previous Articles

Because Miller and Stokes (1963) cite Wright and employ causal diagrams and equations superficially similar to path equations, readers may overlook the fact that their treatment was *not* equivalent to path analysis. Instead, they employed a "variance apportioning algorithm" inspired by Wright's approach, but developed by Stokes from different axioms.[35]

The validity of these axioms is a dead issue because Stokes states that he has since gone through "enough of the literature of econometrics to see that Wright's formulas were strictly implied by the structural equations and restrictions on disturbances which I accepted as true of our model."[36]

The formulas in the original article differ from path equations in two respects: (*a*) The Stokes equations relate the unknown coefficients to *squared* correlation coefficients. (*b*) The Stokes equations omit terms that attribute a part of a total correlation between two variables to the existence of a common cause.

Results of this method differ from those of path analysis. Under the Stokes method, Model IV (in which the representative's preferences influence his perceptions) appeared preferable to Model III, the other theory Miller and Stokes evaluated. Furthermore, the coefficients they derived attribute much more causal importance to the path through perceptions than to the two paths through attitudes combined. A path analysis *using the same data* also selects Model IV over Model III, but path coefficients assign nearly equal importance to the two inter-

34. Stokes (1971) suggests such use of "the method of instrumental variables." He does not, however, propose any specific variables. See also Alker (1969).
35. Even such an authority as Blalock (1967a), in discussing Miller and Stokes' article, expressed the belief that they had used path coefficients.
36. Donald Stokes, letter to the author, 1970.

vening variables, with a slight edge to attitudes over perceptions, contrary to the Miller–Stokes conclusion.[37]

Cnudde and McCrone (1966), in reanalyzing the Miller–Stokes study, proposed using the Simon–Blalock method to infer the "correct" model; the Stokes technique could then measure the importance of different paths within that model. Since introductions to path analysis for social scientists were just beginning to appear when Cnudde and McCrone wrote their article, and since the Stokes technique is not equivalent to path analysis, it is understandable that they thought two methods necessary. As I noted in chapter 5, however, the Simon–Blalock method is merely a weak form of path analysis. Normally, it is more economical to test models directly from path coefficients. The path analytic test has the additional advantage that one can detect immediately any postulated causal connections that can be trimmed.

The inferiority of the Simon–Blalock method is also made evident by the later study of Forbes and Tufte (1968). In challenging Cnudde and McCrone, they used the Simon–Blalock technique to show that at least three models (IIIA, IV, V) are compatible with the data. Consequently, they felt impelled to take an agnostic position on substantive issues. Had they calculated coefficients, they could have learned that acceptable models agree on key points, as I shall now demonstrate.

Substantive Implications

Although none of the six theories tested can claim undisputed validity, and although other conceivable models have not been considered, it may nevertheless be worthwhile to look at substantive implications of the two unrejected models.

37. Recall that correlations used by Miller and Stokes were not corrected for attenuation, whereas those employed in this chapter are corrected. As we have seen, a path analysis using the *corrected* correlations does *not* show Model IV superior to Model III, though it does trim a path from Model III. Furthermore, perceptions are more important when corrected coefficients are used. (See below.)

If they offer qualitatively similar answers to questions of interest, then one might be willing to accept their points of agreement as tentative conclusions.[38]

Three questions will be considered : (*a*) Does the representative respond directly more to her perceptions of constituency desires or to her own preferences? Or, as the question was posed by Miller and Stokes, does she tend to act according to the Burkeian or the instructed-delegate models of representation? (*b*) Does constituency influence over congressional voting operate more by candidate selection or by the representative's conformity to the perceived wishes of voters? (*c*) Who has more power over the representative's vote—the congressperson or the constituency?

Each question will be posed in terms of causal paths in Models IIIA and IV; and answers will be derived from path coefficients calculated above for each model.

Trustee or Delegate? This question can be answered easily by assessing the immediate effects of X_2 and U_3 on the outcome, Y_4. In both models, this means a comparison of d_{42} and d_{43}:

Model	d_{42}	d_{43}
IIIA	.611	.329
IV	.613	.326

As interpreted by both models, the evidence shows the representative responding much more to his perceptions of constituency preferences than to his own attitudes. Representatives act primarily as their constituencies' delegates when voting on civil-rights questions.

This finding does not necessarily imply that the main channel of true constituency influence is through the congressperson's perceptions. His perceptions may be inaccurate, perhaps reflecting his own preferences more heavily than constituents' true attitudes. This possibility is assessed in answering the next question.

38. Boudon (1968:211) suggests this strategy.

The Key Intervening Variable. The relative importance of X_2 and U_3 as intervening variables between U_1 and Y_4 is given by adding for each variable the compound path coefficients of all paths in which it is causally prior to, or independent of, the other variable:

Model	Formula	Result
IIIA	$X_2: d_{21}d_{42} + d_{21}d_{32}d_{43}$	.607
	$U_3: —$	0
IV	$X_2: d_{21}d_{42}$	.340
	$U_3: d_{31}d_{43} + d_{31}d_{23}d_{42}$	.275

Both theories agree that the more important intervening variable is X_2, implying that voters influence representatives more through members' reasonably accurate perceptions of their desires than through selection of candidates whose views correspond to their own. The theories differ in the weight given the two mechanisms. Model IIIA assumes that candidate selection is totally inoperative, while Model IV gives it a weight not much less than it gives the perceptual mechanism.

Who is More Powerful? We have previously rejected a simple power-comparison theory (Model I), in which preferences of both constituency and representative were exogenous. Some impact of U_1 on U_3 is assumed in both unrejected models. Nevertheless, it is possible to assess the relative power of the representative and her constituents by treating the residual, R_c, as the true preference variable for the congressperson.[39] Her power is then given by the total effect of R_c on Y_4; the power of the constituency, by the total effect of U_1 on Y_4.

Model	Actor	Formula	Actor's Power
IIIA	Constituency	$d_{21}d_{42} + d_{21}d_{32}d_{43}$	.607
	Representative	$d_{3c}d_{43}$	.290
IV	Constituency	$d_{21}d_{42} + d_{31}d_{43}$ $+ d_{31}d_{23}d_{42}$	.615
	Representative	$d_{3c}d_{43} + d_{3c}d_{23}d_{42}$	.478

39. See chapter 7 and figure 7.1 above.

Both models concur in giving greater power to the constituency.

Summary. With regard to our three questions, then, the two unrejected ' models exhibit a strong qualitative consensus: Both suggest that, in the area of civil rights, the representative votes primarily as his constituency's delegate; that candidate selection is a secondary or even inoperative channel of constituency influence; and that more power lies with the constituency than with the representative. These conclusions have obvious practical importance. Nevertheless, their limitations should be stressed, especially in view of incautious generalizations in some earlier articles. Only six models out of hundreds possible have been evaluated; models employing other variables have not been considered; and the data pertain to only one issue during a single session of Congress.

9 SYMMETRY AND ASYMMETRY IN POWER RELATIONS

Whether to conceive of power as symmetric or asymmetric has inspired confusion and debate. Blau (1964:117) expresses the prevailing position that power is "inherently asymmetrical." But to Neustadt (1960:43), "real power is reciprocal"; and Lasswell and Kaplan (1950:201) believe that "power cannot be conceived as a unilateral relationship." Others take intermediate positions—Van Doorn (1963:9–10) says power can vary "from an almost completely unilateral relation to one almost purely bilateral."[1]

Similar controversy divides theorists concerned with statistical causal modeling. (This parallelism is additional evidence for the isomorphism of power and causation.) Systems of simultaneous equations, in which variables are mutually dependent, are common in econometrics and statistics. Disagreement arises over the causal interpretation of such relations. One extreme is represented by Juster (1970), who redefines causality so that it applies between simultaneously interdependent variables. Strotz and Wold (1960) advocate the opposite position, restricting causality to recursive systems.

1. Other comments can be found in Oppenheim (1961:104ff.); Singer (1963); Dahlstrom (1966:270–73); Etzioni (1967:317–18, 332–33); Wrong (1968: 673–76); and Nagel (1968:135–37).
   My early article uses the word "power" too loosely. The effects a weaker actor may have upon a stronger cannot generally be construed as power, because they are not necessarily the consequence of the weaker actor's preferences. Merelman (1968) makes the same mistake. In an odd defense of "pluralism," he argues that whenever elites coerce other groups, "we may also infer ... that the elite has been coerced into exerting sanctions. Initiators have severely restricted the elite's alternatives. Should we not consider this situation evidence of the strength of the initiators as well as of the elite?"

In their view, simultaneous equations can be interpreted causally only as imperfect representations of underlying recursive processes.

This debate may seem metaphysical, as both sides admit the necessity of simultaneous systems and sometimes interpret them in causal language, but the opposed positions probably have different theoretical consequences. Those who believe in asymmetric causality are more likely to remodel simultaneous relations in recursive form. Their working assumption about causality may then be justified to the extent that it produces improved understanding and more powerful theories.[2]

My reliance on Simon's definition implies acceptance of the asymmetric view of causality.[3] Nevertheless, with Alker (1969:9), I recognize that "political reality obviously includes a number of symmetrical, reciprocal influence relationships: for example, bargaining, the exchange of leadership for support, and arms races. If these can be studied from a causal point of view, a major difficulty in applying causal inference techniques to political phenomena will be overcome." Accordingly, this chapter examines four types of symmetrical power. The primary purpose is to reanalyze each type to restore the asymmetric ordering of preferences and outcomes, which confers the advantages of unambiguous causal interpretation and easier estimation procedures. In two instances, however, we are forced to admit that nonrecursive structures may be needed. Problems in estimating and interpreting them are briefly discussed.

INTERCURSIVE POWER

Once one grants that power is not simply a relation between actors, but instead must be defined with respect to specified outcomes, then it becomes easy to recognize and analyze the

2. For examples, see Strotz and Wold (1960).
3. Simon's position is not identical with that of Strotz and Wold, who contrast his "vector causality" (defined for block recursive systems) with their own "explicit causality" (limited to pure recursive structures).

type of reciprocal influence that Wrong (1968:674), following Geiger, calls "intercursive" power. In this common class of power relations, "the control of one person or group over the other with reference to a particular scope is balanced by the control of the other over a different scope." Intercursive power often results from bargaining or exchange. As Banfield (1961:242) notes, "if, for example, [Mayor Daley] has control over a state senator in a certain matter, it may be because he has given the senator control over him in another matter." Similarly, Mayor Lee of New Haven surrendered power over appointments to Democratic party boss Arthur Barbieri in return for a free hand in determining urban renewal policies (Talbot, 1967).

Thus, power relations that in one sense are mutual, with two actors influencing each other, can be analyzed into two asymmetric causal relations, in which the actors' preferences separately determine different outcomes: $U_a \rightarrow Y_1$ and $U_b \rightarrow Y_2$.[4]

This analysis dissolves one of Dahl's paradoxes of antici-pated reactions. Imagine, Dahl (1968) suggests, a senator who, without any previous action by the president, "regularly votes now in a way he thinks will insure the President's favor later," hoping to receive a judgeship should he lose the next election. If the president does eventually appoint the senator to the bench, "it appears, paradoxically, that it is not the President who controls the Senator, but the Senator who controls the President—i.e., it is the Senator who, by his loyal behavior, induces the President to appoint him to a Federal court."

This situation is puzzling only if (*a*) social causation is thought to require temporal sequence of behaviors, and (*b*) influence is treated purely as a relation between actors. If instead one treats preferences as the causal variable in social influence and distinguishable outcomes or responses as the object of power, then the solution is easily perceived. The senator does indeed influence the president—with respect to

---

4. Contrast the treatment of symbiosis in Juster (1970: 83).

judiciary selection, and the president also influences the senator—with respect to votes. The relationship is simply an exchange of influence over distinct outcomes.

SHARED POWER OVER A SINGLE OUTCOME

The definition of power as causation of outcomes by preferences is not essential to recognition of intercursive power, but it does help reveal asymmetry in a second class of superficially reciprocal power relations.

After defining power as causation of behavior by behavior, Simon (1953) attempts to deal with two types of influence situations that seem to lack the asymmetry he requires: (*a*) power in the presence of "feedback"; and (*b*) the rule of anticipated reactions.

Feedback

Simon illustrates the kind of feedback he has in mind with the following example: "Our dictator makes a decision, and if he is sensitive to public approval and disapproval, then we will observe in sequence: (1) the decision, (2) subsequent changes in behavior of the subjects, (3) expressions of approval or disapproval by the subjects, and (4) modifications in the decision if it proves to be unpopular." In a static behaviorist analysis, the situation must be depicted as reciprocal. Dictator's behavior (B_1) influences subjects' behavior (B_2), and vice versa (figure 9.1).

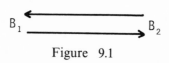

$$B_1 \qquad\qquad\qquad B_2$$

Figure   9.1

If the variables are defined for different time periods, $B_i(t)$, asymmetric causation is restored (figure 9.2).

$$B_1(0) \longrightarrow B_2(1) \longrightarrow B_1(2) \longrightarrow \ \cdot \ \cdot$$

Figure 9.2

Observation of the separate influence links is, however, possible only if a reasonable time lag exists between each pair of behaviors in the sequence.

Anticipated Reactions

Simon next admits "an even graver difficulty." When influence occurs through anticipated reactions, "the time lags upon which we depend for measurement may be destroyed." When reactions are anticipated, Simon believes, "the possibility of measuring the separate links in the chain of influence" depends entirely "on the presence of some ignorance in the system." If one actor errs in his anticipation, the other will react unfavorably, and a temporally distinct sequence of behaviors will occur. Using Simon's definition of power, however, one is unable even to conceptualize, let alone observe, influence exerted through *correctly* anticipated reactions.

Simon's behaviorism led him to neglect the forest for the trees. In studying influence, attention should not generally focus upon exact sequences of action and response. Interaction processes are common in social influence, but they are not essential to its definition, occurrence, or observation. Mutually responsive behaviors should be treated as intervening variables between the truly essential variables at either end of the causal sequence—the preferences of each actor and the ultimate outcome. Behavioral sequences of the type Simon describes are a way of negotiating the final outcome, as each party makes evident to the other its own preferences, capabilities, and intended responses. Observation of interaction may be useful in detecting preferences and in deciding causal priority, but it is not invariably necessary. If interaction disappears altogether, as when reactions are correctly anticipated, influence can still exist; and it may be possible to infer and measure it, using methods we have previously examined.

How should one model the situations that perplex Simon? Both are instances of two actors sharing influence over a single outcome (figure 9.3).

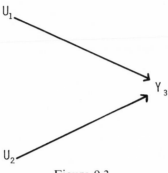

Figure 9.3

This representation preserves the only essential asymmetry—
the causal ordering of preferences and outcomes. Between the
actors, there may exist balance and interaction (they share
power over the outcome, and they react to each other in
determining it), or asymmetry and imbalance (as when one has
more influence than the other; or when the outcome is the
behavior of one, partially controlled by the other). But it is
important to distinguish the asymmetry of events, interaction,
and social relations from the asymmetry of variables in a model.
Only the latter is a defining characteristic of power.

The analysis so far has assumed that preferences themselves
are causally prior to the outcome and independent of each
other. Can the asymmetry of causal ordering be maintained
when preferences instead (*a*) reciprocally determine each other,
or (*b*) are altered by feedback from outcomes they supposedly
cause?

INTERACTING PREFERENCES

Frequently, both behavioral interaction and anticipation of
reactions lead to mutual adjustment of preferences, through
persuasion, social comparison, empathy, love, hatred. Since
preferences are essential in power models, interacting preferences entail reciprocal influence of a basic type. Figure 9.4
represents the simplest static interacting-preferences model:

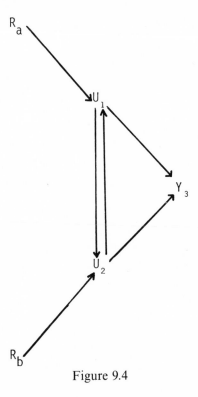

Figure 9.4

Despite the presence of the reciprocal relation between U_1 and U_2, this block-recursive model retains some of the asymmetry of causal ordering. Both preference variables are causally prior to the outcome. As the model stands, coefficients linking the preferences to each other are not identifiable; but any of four stratagems can make some degree of power measurement possible.

Partitioning the Model

The relation between U_1 and U_2 may be treated as an unanalyzed correlation (figure 9.5).

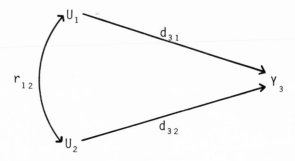

Figure 9.5

As a consequence of what Boudon (1967:120–21) calls the "principle of partition," the structural coefficients d_{31} and d_{32} will be the same, whether the U_1–U_2 relation is estimated as two separate causal paths or left unanalyzed. These coefficients are the only power measures obtained, however, when the indirect paths through each other's preferences are not causally interpreted.

Combination of Variables

If the reciprocal relation is positive and very strong relative to the time period over which it has operated, the two actors can be treated as a single source of influence. This is permissible because multicollinearity is likely and the two preference variables will have attained a stable equilibrium relation (Ando, Fisher, and Simon, 1963).[5]

Introduction of Lags

If preference interaction occurs over time, and separate observations of preferences at different periods are possible, then the two variables may be lagged in a manner similar to that suggested by Simon for behavioral interaction (figure 9.6). This device makes the reciprocal system recursive.

5. Cf. also Abelson (1964) and Harary (1959), theorems 9 and 11.

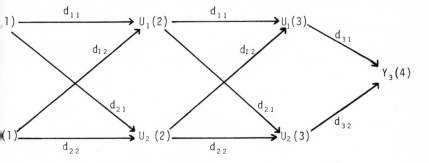

Figure 9.6

Ambiguity is introduced, however, into the meaning and measurement of power. Each actor now has several distinct preferences, defined for different points in time. Should measures of influence on the outcome start from initial preferences, intervening preferences, or final preferences? Measures of power may vary depending on which are adopted.[6] Suppose that d_{31} far exceeds d_{32}, but that at each earlier stage d_{12} and d_{22} are high, while d_{11} and d_{21} are low. Then the immediate power of actor 1 over Y_3 is great, but the less malleable actor 2 may have greater influence over the long term. The influence relation from 1968 to 1972 between antiwar activists (actor 2) and the Democratic party elite (actor 1) roughly fits this pattern. If Senator Muskie had won the presidency in 1972, the party elite would have decided Vietnam policy (Y_3), but their preferences were strongly affected by the efforts of protestors on whom they had no influence.[7]

To measure power in a system like figure 9.6 would demand data rarely available outside the laboratory. Nevertheless,

6. Cervin (1957) develops a mathematical model in which the weaker party's ultimate effect on the stronger is in the opposite direction from that which the weaker initially prefers, although in each period its influence is in a preferred direction! In French's model, effect of initial preferences on the ultimate outcome depends more on structural position, than on direct power over other individuals (French, 1956:191–93; and Harary, 1959: 174–76).

7. Cf. French (1956), theorem 3.

recognition that reciprocal influence occurs through dynamic recursive processes should promote better theory. Excellent formal models mathematically depicting influence in this way have already appeared.[8]

Nonrecursive Estimation

Nonexperimental empirical researchers, when confronted by interacting preferences, will ordinarily be forced to estimate reciprocal links in a static nonrecursive structure. If the simultaneously observed values can be reasonably considered the equilibrium outcomes of an asymmetric process, coefficients relating the two preferences may be viewed as measures of power or influence.[9]

To identify the reciprocal paths in a model like figure 9.4, the investigator must observe two or more additional variables, each known to affect U_1 or U_2, but not both. In figure 9.7, normal path algorithms do not yield a suitable measure of the actors' influence on Y_3, because they omit the "reverberation" effect of the reciprocal preference interaction. Instead, the path coefficient measures of total influence are amplified by a factor resulting from this interaction. In this example, the total power of actor 1 is given by $(d_{14} + d_{1a})$ $(d_{31} + d_{21}d_{32})/(1 - d_{12}d_{21})$. The measure of actor 2's power is $(d_{25} + d_{2b})(d_{32} + d_{12}d_{31})/(1 - d_{12}d_{21})$.[10]

8. See articles cited in footnotes 5, 6, and 7 in this chapter, plus Cervin and Henderson (1961) and Taylor (1968).

9. In the sense that, if we (or nature) intervened to determine U_1 exogenously, the coefficient relating it to U_2 would enable us to predict the value of U_2 when (and if) equilibrium is restored. Without knowing the dynamic relations, however, we cannot predict the values of the variables through time as they approach equilibrium. Cf. Strotz and Wold (1960).

10. These measures are taken from the "reduced-form" equation for Y_3, which expresses Y_3 as a function of residuals and the predetermined variables X_4 and X_5, omitting U_1 and U_2. Use of the method for a similar example is explained in Duncan, Haller and Portes (1968). Note that if either d_{12} or d_{21} is negative, the power measures are reduced, not amplified. If either is zero, the measures are, appropriately, the same as in a recursive model. The first factors in each expression discount each preference to reflect the fact they are partly nonautonomous; i.e., influenced by another preference. See chapter 7 above.

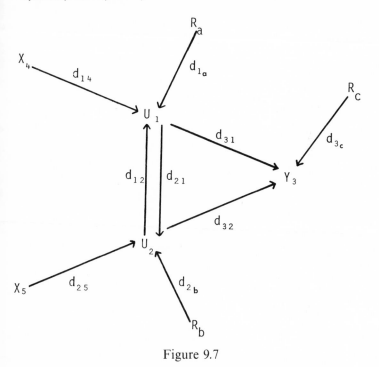

Figure 9.7

FEEDBACK FROM OUTCOMES TO PREFERENCES

The most fundamental type of symmetry occurs when outcomes feed back to affect preferences. For example, though constituency preferences (U_1) influence congressional votes (Y_2), in the long run positions of representatives may also affect constituents' attitudes (a possibility ignored in the constituency influence literature). Represented statically, such feedback destroys all asymmetry; the variables are no longer causally ordered (figure 9.8).

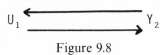

Figure 9.8

There are two ways to restore asymmetry, but each requires that power be interpreted in a modified or restricted fashion.

Lagging of Variables

Using the now-familiar procedure, the variables can be lagged (figure 9.9).

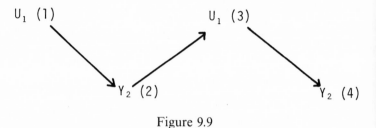

Figure 9.9

This introduces an ambiguity to the meaning of power similar to that discussed in the preceding section. Between adjoining time periods, the measure of actor 1's influence over Y_2 is unequivocal. Over a longer time, however, several measures are possible, just as when preferences interact. In this case, however, if the coefficients d_{21} are roughly constant, it seems reasonable to accept their value as *the* measure of the actor's power.

Approximation to Recursiveness

If the feedback from outcomes to preferences is relatively slight, then in the short run, it is permissible to ignore it and to treat the system as recursive.[11] The length of the "short run" is inversely related to both the magnitude of feedback and the accuracy demanded of one's results. As the time span of a study increases, the impact of even slight short-run feedback can become substantial—indeed, virtually unrelated to the size of the short-run coefficient (Ando et al., p. 88). Therefore, if one accepts the ecologists' premise that most variables are

11. This paragraph is based on Ando, Fisher, and Simon (1963).

ultimately interrelated, it is essential to choose appropriately restricted time periods over which to gather data used in estimating recursive models.

Nonrecursive Estimation

Finally, as with interacting preferences, the reciprocal relations between preference and outcome can be estimated as part of a static, nonrecursive model. Again, causal interpretation depends on assuming equilibrium observations and an underlying recursive process.

10 *POWER AND CONFLICT*

Next to power, conflict is perhaps the most frequently used term in political science; and in the other social sciences, it probably appears even more often than power. Since so much research and theorizing center on these concepts, to explore relations between them may facilitate a useful transfer of findings.

EFFECTS OF CONFLICT ON POWER

Does Power Presuppose Conflict?

Most writers believe that conflict is a necessary condition of power.[1] At least one, Frey (1971), disagrees. In what sense, if any, does my conception of power presuppose the existence of conflict?

Axelrod (1970) distinguishes two types of conflict–conflictful behavior (e.g., quarrels, strikes, wars) and conflict of preferences (which he calls conflict of interest). Conflictful behavior is *not* a precondition of power as I define it, because preferences can determine outcomes without overt struggle when reactions are correctly anticipated, when power resources are well known, when one actor totally dominates another, when information or incentives are cleverly manipulated.

The relation of power to conflict of interest is more complicated. Assume that the correlation between two actors' preferences is a rough inverse measure of the degree of conflict of interest between them.[2] Because of the statistical problem

1. Examples include Weber (1947), Bierstedt (1950), Dahl (1957), Bachrach and Baratz (1963), Kahn (1964), and Etzioni (1968: 317).
2. Axelrod's axiomatically derived measure of conflict of interest (CI) is quite different from the corelation of preferences in path analytic power measurement: (*a*) CI is defined for only a single outcome event; the corre-

of multicollinearity, if preferences correlate perfectly, it will be impossible to distinguish the influence of the two actors; and if the correlation is high but not perfect, significant measures of individual influence will be hard to obtain.[3] In this sense, conflict of preferences is a necessary condition of power (or, more strictly, of power measurement). This conclusion must, however, be qualified in two ways.

First, as I noted in chapter 7, correspondence of desires may itself result from influence. Indirect influence does not negate the relation between conflict and power, however, for one must infer that the two actors' preferences *would* conflict were one not influencing the other.

Second, in the absence of indirect influence, actors with highly similar preferences can be treated as a single entity. This is permissible even if the actors are otherwise distinguishable, and even if no obvious coordination, alliance, or conspiracy exists between them.[4] Without conflict of preferences

---

lation depends on all events within an outcome category. (*b*) CI depends on all Pareto-optimal possible states of the outcome event; the correlation is computed from preference values for states that actually occur.

It is conceivable that preferences for actual outcomes might correlate + 1, even though CI for each event is high; or, conversely, that each CI might be zero while preferences correlate negatively. Such possibilities seem highly improbable. It is more likely that the correlation of preferences will correspond closely to average CI across the events in an outcome category. This is what I assume in treating the correlation as a measure of conflict and agreement.

3. On multicollinearity, see page 74 above. Cf. also Dahl (1958): "One can test for differences in influence only where there are cases of differences in initial preferences."

4. Although they performed no statistical analysis, the conclusion of Marc Pilisuk and Tom Hayden (1965) applies this principle: "Our concept is not that American society contains a ruling military-industrial complex. Our concept is more nearly that American society *is* a military-industrial complex."

An alternative strategy, suggested by Gerrit Wolf, is to redefine the outcome variable into two or more new variables, with respect to one or more of which the high correlation does not obtain. Thus, many American corporations and labor unions are part of a military-industrial complex with respect to foreign policy and defense issues, but they conflict over domestic issues and wage policy.

the relationship between the actors will not involve power, but a relation of power or control may exist between them jointly and an outcome. Missing will be the threats, tension, strategy, bargaining, manipulation associated with competition for power; and attempts to apportion their joint power between them will be futile.

Covariation of Conflict and Individual Power

It is interesting to observe the magnitude of influence coefficients as the correlation between preferences varies. Consider a two-person situation in which the outcome is entirely caused by the actors' preferences (figure 10.1).

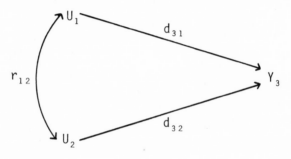

Figure 10.1

According to the basic variance-apportioning formula (equation 5.20),

$$d_{31}{}^2 + d_{32}{}^2 + 2d_{31}d_{32}r_{12} = 1 \tag{10.1}$$

One can immediately see that as r_{12} increases, d_{31} or d_{32} or both must decrease; and when r_{12} declines, d_{31} or d_{32} or both must increase. In short, measures of individual power vary directly with conflict of preferences. The gain (loss) in the individual coefficients is offset by a loss (gain) in the third term of the equation, which reflects the joint power of the two actors. Thus, not only is individual power unmeasurable without conflicting preferences, but also the amount of individually assignable influence varies directly with the amount of conflict.

This conclusion is, of course, purely mathematical, and it depends on the assumption that total power remains constant.[5] In many empirical situations, total power is no doubt inversely related to conflict of preferences, so that increased agreement might result in greater individual power for both actors.

Benefit, Conflict, and Power

Another interesting result concerns the effect of conflict of preferences on actors' benefit from an outcome. A plausible measure of *benefit* is the correlation between an actor's preference and the outcome variable. Following the paths in figure 10.1, it is easy to see that, although an actor's benefit varies directly with his own power, it also depends upon the power of the other actor, unless the correlation between their preferences is zero:

$$\text{Actor 1's Benefit} = r_{13} = d_{31} + r_{12}d_{32} \qquad (10.2)$$

Because of the second term in equation 10.2, benefit varies directly with agreement (as measured by r_{12}), assuming the other's power (d_{32}) to be positive. On the other hand, as the preceding subsection showed, individual power can vary inversely with agreement; and this power (measured by d_{31} and d_{32}) also affects benefit. Which effect will be greater cannot be stated a priori. But it does appear that a paradoxical result is possible: An actor may benefit from an increase in agreement even though it causes him to lose individual power. Conversely, greater conflict of preferences may be accompanied by both a rise in individual power and a fall in benefit.

Subjective Power

The power measures developed in this book are intended to gauge actors' objective influence upon outcomes, not their

5. In equation 10.1, total power is at its maximum, which is one. For an explanation of "total power," see the second part of this chapter.

subjective feeling of power or powerlessness. This distinction is important for two reasons. Some procedures for measuring "power" actually tap subjective feelings of influence (e.g., the questionnaires used by Tannenbaum and his associates in constructing their "control graph"[6]). Second, subjective power is undoubtedly a significant variable in its own right (e.g., as a determinant of confidence, discontent, alienation).

An exploration of the possible causes of subjective power is beyond the scope of a methodological work, but one speculation is worth noting in the present context. It is conceivable that subjective power may sometimes depend more on benefit than on objective power. For example, an actor who vigorously seeks to influence an outcome may tend to attribute any correspondence of outcome and desire to her own influence, even if her objective causal effect only partly accounts for the correspondence.

As we have seen, objective power and benefit can vary in opposite directions as the degree of conflict of preferences changes. Therefore, depending on which has the greater effect on subjective power (assuming either affects it), subjective power may be greatest in either a high-conflict or a low-conflict system.

IS TOTAL POWER FIXED OR VARIABLE?

We have been examining the effect of conflict on power. Now we ask how close the relation is between pursuit of power and the arousal of conflict.

Any value is more likely to evoke conflict if its supply is fixed (Deutsch, 1966). As Parsons asks, is "a gain in power by a unit *A* . . . in the nature of the case the cause of a corresponding loss of power by other units, *B*, *C*, *D*?"

Parsons was perhaps the first theorist to raise the "zero-sum" issue with respect to power.[7] In an attack on C. Wright Mills' book *The Power Elite*, Parsons (1957) accused Mills of im-

6. For citations, see footnote 9 below.
7. The terms fixed-sum or constant-sum are preferable.

plicitly adopting a fixed sum view of power. This conception, he argued, led Mills to focus on power distribution, at the expense of neglecting power "production," which Parsons believes necessary to accomplish communal as well as particularistic goals.[8]

In later, more theoretical papers, Parsons (1963a, 1963b) returned to the fixed-sum problem, citing it as one of three principal issues in the conceptualization of power. His emphasis on the variability of power has since been picked up by Pye (1967) and Huntington (1968), who consider the absolute level of power in a society an important factor in political development and a key dimension along which polities may be compared.

Interest in the zero-sum question also developed, apparently independently, in organization theory. Tannenbaum and other organizational psychologists of the Michigan group, utilizing a survey device called the "control graph," discovered that in some companies employees at all hierarchical levels believe they exert strong influence over decisions, while in other companies, workers at all levels perceive themselves as having little influence. According to a fixed-sum view of power, high influence for supervisors should correlate with low influence for workers, and vice versa—a pattern found in some, but not all, organizations studied. The discrepant cases led the researchers to propose that total power in an organization can vary, so that a group within an organization might increase its influence without decreasing the influence of any other group.[9]

The optimism implicit in this position is echoed by others who espouse the variable-sum conception. Wheeler (1968) sees in the expandability of power an argument against national sovereignty and in favor of an international political

---

8. Oddly enough, the same charge was hurled from the opposing side in the pluralist-elitist controversy, when Gitlin (1965) accused Dahl of harboring a zero-sum conception of power.
9. See Tannenbaum (1957, 1961), Tannenbaum and Georgopolous (1957), Tannenbaum and Kahn (1957), and Lammers (1967).

order. Marcuse (1964), to whom power is a negative value, hopes for an eventual reduction in the overall level of power. Most theorists take it for granted that power will always be positively valued, but they believe its increase can reduce conflict. The analogy is often drawn (most thoroughly by Lammers, 1967) to the taming effect of economic growth on the class struggle, the diversion of attention from distribution to production.

Among theorists who discuss the fixed-sum question there exists some disagreement.[10] Rapoport (1960:110) considers power a "conservative quantity" (i.e., fixed in amount). Deutsch (1966) says that power is expandable up to a limit, after which "the allocation of actual power becomes a fixed-sum game." He has also commented that, of Lasswell's eight basic values, power is the most likely to lead to fixed-sum situations.[11] Most writers share Deutsch's general position, but many imply that the ceiling on total power is not so close as he suggests.

The path analytic framework, coupled with the definition of power as causation by preferences, can illuminate this issue. In the ensuing analysis, I first develop measures for the total amount of power exercised over an outcome. These measures enable us to discern sources of variation in total power; and they suggest that, depending upon the nature of the outcome and the empirical situation, total power can be potentially unlimited, variable up to a limit, or fixed.

Measuring Total Power

At first, it might appear that the total amount of power exercised over an outcome should be measured simply by adding together the influence coefficients of all actors whose

10. One quarrel over the issue broke up a book-writing partnership. Hickson (1970), in his review of *The Distribution of Authority in Formal Organizations*, by Dalton, Barnes, and Zaleznik, reports that Dalton and Barnes wrote a separate chapter when they could not agree with Zaleznik over whether or not power in organizations is fixed in sum.

11. In a Yale political theory seminar, February 16, 1967.

preferences affect the outcome. A sufficient objection to this approach is that the three possible influence coefficients can rank differently the amounts of total power in two or more situations. Consider the path coefficient and the squared path coefficient as applied to figure 10.1. Suppose that in Situation A, $d_{31} = .8$ and $d_{32} = .6$. These path coefficients sum to 1.4; their squares sum to 1.0. Imagine that in Situation B, actor 1 gains all the power: $d_{31} = 1.0$ and $d_{32} = 0$. According to the sum of path coefficients, total power has decreased from 1.4 to 1.0. According to the sum of squared coefficients, total power remains 1.0.

Which measure is more suitable? The definition of power as causation by preferences gives no reason to think that total power has declined from Situation A to Situation B. The outcome remains entirely caused by preferences. This reasoning suggests that *the total variance explained by preferences* should be adopted as the essential meaning of the total amount of power exercised over an outcome.

Does this imply that the sum of squared path coefficients is the best measure of total power? Not generally. The preceding example is a limiting case in that it assumes preferences to be uncorrelated. The general variance-apportioning formula (equation 5.20) includes terms that reflect correlations among causal variables:

$$s_j^2 = 1 = \sum_i d_{ji}^2 + 2 \sum_{\substack{ik \\ i \neq k}} d_{ji}d_{jk}r_{ik} + d_{jj}^2 \qquad (10.3)$$

Two correlated preference variables, U_i and U_k, jointly account for that part of the variance measured by $2d_{ji}d_{jk}r_{ik}$. Since the correlation is not causally analyzed, we cannot attribute this effect to either actor separately; but it certainly is included in the total variance explained by preferences.[12] Therefore, a measure of total power should incorporate all such terms, in addition to squared path coefficients.

12. These joint power terms correspond fairly well to what Nardin (1973) calls the "aggregative" concept of power, which presupposes agreement. The d_{ji}^2 can be identified with his "distributive" concept.

Power models can also include causal variables other than preferences. Figure 10.2 depicts a model with a nonpreference causal variable, X_3:

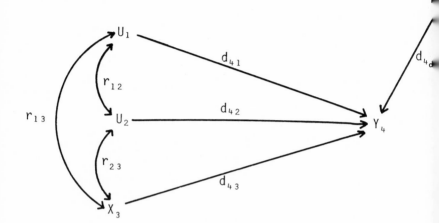

Figure 10.2

Clearly, $d_{43}{}^2$ does not belong in the measure of total power, but what about terms involving correlations between non-preference and preference variables ($2d_{41}d_{43}r_{13}$ and $2d_{42}d_{43}r_{23}$)? Somewhat arbitrarily, I prefer not to include them, because they represent variance that cannot be unequivocally attributed to preferences. Others might follow the opposite policy or compromise by including half of each term.

We have arrived at a general formula for total power, *TP*, in models without intervening variables :[13]

$$TP = \sum_i d_{ji}{}^2 + \sum_{\substack{ik \\ i \neq k}} 2d_{ji}d_{jk}r_{ik} \qquad (10.4)$$

13. Total power measures for models with intervening variables can be derived by following suggestions in chapter 5, footnote 22, above.

where the index i represents all causal preference variables, and the ik are all pairs of causal preference variables.[14]

It is now easy to answer the original question: "Is total power fixed or variable?"

Sources of Variation in Total Power

As figure 10.2 makes evident, variance can be divided into three categories: (a) that accounted for entirely by preferences; (b) that explained entirely or partially by variables other than preferences; and (c) residual variance. Only variance in the first category is included in the measure of total power. Therefore, *total power exercised over an outcome can expand if the causal effect of preferences increases at the expense of unexplained variance and/or nonpreference causes.* Such increases can occur for a variety of reasons—improved skill in exercising power, better communication of preferences, better mobilization and coordination of human energies, reduction of the impact of irrational impulses, and avoidance of unnecessary struggles.

An industrial example can illustrate this possibility. Lammers (1967) suggests that participation by workers in decision making "may boost the joint power of superiors and subordinates alike in that, as a consequence . . . subordinates may become more willing and able to carry out decisions the intended way." The change he envisions can be depicted in path diagrams as a shift from Structure A to Structure B in figure 10.3. The variables have the following meanings:

U_1 = managers' preferences
U_2 = workers' preferences
Y_3 = company policies
Y_4 = actual company performance

14. One can also construct an unstandardized measure of total power (Nagel, 1972: 279–80, 283–85). This reveals an additional source of variation in total power: changes in the absolute range through which power holders can cause outcomes to vary. The unstandardized measure is omitted here, because it depends on the questionable possibility of a determinate scale for measuring preferences. (See chapter 8 above.)

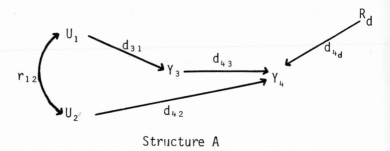

Structure A

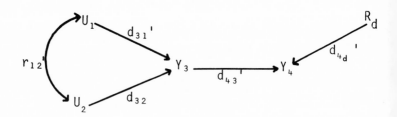

Structure B

Figure 10.3

In A, the preparticipation situation, management controls company policies ($d_{31} = 1$) but has trouble implementing its decisions (d_{43} is low). Implementation depends upon the workers, who express their own preferences in their performance ($d_{42} > 0$), and who also sabotage official policies by non-rational and perhaps self-defeating actions resulting from their formal powerlessness—withholding information, day-dreaming, carelessness. (The influence of these factors is included in d_{4d}.)

By introducing participatory decision making (Structure B), management relinquishes some of its power over policy to the workers ($d_{31}' < d_{31}$ and $d_{32} > 0$). This transfer, Lammers proposes, (1) may augment total power and (2) increase both managers' and workers' influence over implementation.

Hypothesis (1) translates mathematically to:

$$d_{31}'^2 d_{43}'^2 + d_{32}^2 d_{43}'^2 + 2d_{43}'^2 d_{32} d_{31}' r_{12}'$$
$$> d_{31}^2 d_{43}^2 + d_{42}^2 + 2d_{42} d_{31} d_{43} r_{12} \tag{10.8}$$

This is equivalent to:

$$1 - d_{4d}^2 > 1 - d_{4d}^2 \tag{10.9}$$

Hypothesis (2) implies:

$$d_{31}' d_{43}' > d_{31} d_{43} \quad \text{and} \tag{10.10a}$$

$$d_{32} d_{43}' > d_{42} \tag{10.10b}$$

The simultaneous increase in influence of both managers and workers results from the greater effect of company decisions on actual performance $(d_{43}' > d_{43})$, gained by reducing the effect of nonpreference factors $(d_{4d}' < d_{4d})$ as a consequence of giving workers a voice in formal decision making $(d_{32}$ replaces $d_{42})$.[15]

Fluctuations in total power discussed so far pertain to power over a single outcome variable. The notion of total power can be extended to reflect the *number* of outcomes caused by preferences.

Thus a second type of power expansion occurs whenever a new outcome becomes subject, in some degree, to control by individual or group preferences.[16] Until 1969, the annual frequency of flights to the moon did not depend at all upon human desires. Children and presidents alike might dream of space voyages, but neither could realize the wish. Now the question is subject to human choice, and groups with differing preferences compete for power over the decision. Any actor that achieves some degree of influence over moon-flight policy has gained power. Has any actor been deprived of power as a

15. An additional effect of collaborative decision making may be increased agreement between workers and management $(r_{12}' > r_{12})$. This will not reduce total power, and it should increase total benefit; but it may reduce the separate influence of one or both groups.
16. This "second type" is obviously a limiting case of the first, in which preexpansion TP = 0.

consequence? Perhaps—but only if other outcomes have become *less* subject to causation by preferences (as may well have happened in this case, because of diversion of resources).

The space flight example suggests the contribution technological progress can make to power expansion; but organizational and political factors are even more important, especially over short time periods. For example, according to most firsthand observers, mobilization and liberation of human energies in China during its continuing revolution have greatly increased the degree of human control over a vast number of outcomes.[17]

Relation to Ideas of Other Theorists

By now it is evident that Parsons and others who emphasize the variability of total power are in general correct, according to my definition and measures. The second type of power expansion outlined above is potentially open-ended, subject only to whatever limits exist to technological and organizational progress. Those who, like Deutsch, see power as expandable only up to a ceiling are correct with respect to single outcome variables. Finally, when all the variance of an outcome is already caused by preferences or when nonpreference causation and / or residual variance are irreducible, then the constant-sum conception of power is appropriate.

Moon expeditions and Chinese development may suggest to some readers that variations in power have more to do with human conquest of nature than with power as an aspect of social interaction. Although counterexamples are easily produced—e.g., more control over unemployment levels—it is especially easy to imagine power expansion through increasing control of nature.

Deutsch (1970:25), in an ambivalent passage, even flirts with equating variable power to power over nature, and fixed-sum power to social power. The distinction between power over nature and social power is not easy to maintain, however. In

17. See Greene (1961), Snow (1961), Myrdal (1965), or many recent reports.

Lammers' example, expanded human power is gained not at the expense of material nature, but by reducing the influence of nonrational social and organizational factors—human nature, if you will. Furthermore, much of the most significant power is exercised over neither nature nor individuals. Instead, it consists of the influence of persons or groups over joint decision-making mechanisms of which they are members—voting aggregations, alliances, supersystems in general. This is the power of "I" over "us," as opposed to the power of "I" over "you." As in the company policy example, sharing of power over joint decisions is often a prerequisite for effective power over "nature." Thus, Deutsch seems on firmer ground when he decides that "it is possible to increase [social power] to the degree that men expand their capacity to act, to do things, and to coordinate their behavior, or to comply with other people's wishes."

Riker (1964:345), however, speculates that power defined in terms of outcomes "always exists. It cannot be eradicated for it refers to outcomes and, so long as outcomes occur, it exists. If ego runs out of power, still someone else in the n-person system has the ability to influence an outcome." In contrast, "other-oriented" power, defined in terms of the behavior of another actor, may vanish, Riker believes.

The category "outcomes" as used in this book is meant to be flexible enough to include the behavior of other actors, so both of Riker's types are subsumed in my definition of power. Nevertheless, from my perspective, Riker is wrong even with respect to his restricted version of outcomes. Influence lost by one actor may be transferred to causes other than another actor's preferences, or residual variance may increase at the expense of total power. Riker is correct for situations in which an outcome is *necessarily* caused entirely by human preferences. As it happens, his conclusion was a generalization from the Shapley–Shubik voting power analysis, in which the required qualification is met.

Another kind of variation in total power occurs if power is defined to be exercised only over others. Given this restriction, power over an actor contracts and expands in proportion as his behavior is determined by his own or by others' preferences. Whether or not to adopt this limitation is partly a semantic question, and partly a matter of theoretical convenience. Certainly it does no violence to everyday language to refer to autonomy as power over oneself.

Finally, my analysis reveals a questionable premise in the thinking of B. F. Skinner (1953:439), who believes that "to refuse to accept control ... is merely to leave control in other hands." Skinner often uses this conservation-of-power argument to support his well-known plans for scientific, communally organized control of child rearing and socialization. Skinner persistently equates "control" with "causation." A determinist may legitimately believe that all behavior is caused, but at present relatively few behaviors are caused by human preferences. Therefore, Skinner advocates a great increase in power as defined in this book.

11 *CONCLUSION*

The descriptive approach to power advanced in this book may appear unduly restrictive to many readers. Its dependence on outcomes seems to deprive the concept of explanatory and predictive import and to neglect the traditional connotation of power as a potentiality or capability. Ideas that many think indispensable to power analysis are omitted—rewards and punishments, psychological forces, payoffs and costs. Readers troubled by such doubts will, I hope, find them allayed by the first part of this chapter.

EXPLANATORY POWER ANALYSIS

Clear thinking about power requires recognition of the difference between descriptive and explanatory analysis. Progress in power research depends on understanding how the two relate. The present framework enables one to appreciate both the distinction and the interface.

Two Levels of Theory

It is fashionable to contend that development of "theory" is a precondition for advances in defining or measuring power. March (1966) says, "The concept of power must be embedded in a model and the validity of the model is a prerequisite to the utility of the concept.... The measurement problem and the model problem have to be solved simultaneously." Bell et al. (1969 : 121) echo the theme : "Concept formation itself depends upon theory formation."

Unfortunately, proponents of this view pay little attention to distinguishing levels and types of theories required for different purposes. As we shall see, rudimentary theories are adequate for some uses, while complicated and advanced models are essential for other applications.

My power definition and measures do conform to the dicta of March and company. To apply them, one must posit a *theory of the outcome*, in which the outcome is explained, partially or entirely, by causally prior preferences.

Note that this indispensable theory is really quite simple. The only variables it must include are preferences and the outcome itself. The explanation such a theory affords is minimal. If the causal specification is justifiable and coefficient estimates are significant, one can infer that events occurred as they did because various actors had certain preferences—an "explanation" unlikely to satisfy anyone with normal curiosity. To add to this the clause "and because power was distributed in the amount d_{ji} to each actor i" is to state a tautology.

Outcome theories may also lack predictive utility. A structure of power coefficients estimated using data from the past permits reasonable predictions of the future only if coefficients remain approximately constant. Empirical power structures may or may not be sufficiently static; one cannot decide on the basis of the outcome theory alone. The "predictions" permitted by descriptive theories are mere projections.

Satisfying explanation and insightful prediction depend upon the construction of *theories of power*—models in which coefficients themselves are endogenous.

An ideal theory of power would generate numerical power coefficients, given the values of parameters and exogenous variables. Power coefficients could then be derived in two ways—*deductively* from the theory of power, and *inductively* from outcome and preference observations and the theory of the outcome. It would then be possible to test and improve theories of power by comparing theoretical coefficients with empirical estimates.[1]

1. My distinction of inductive and deductive derivations of power coefficients is similar to Simon's (1954) discussion of direct and indirect power measures: "Direct measurements of influence are obtained when we can observe the ratio of change in behavior of influencee to change in behavior of influencer. If, starting with such measurements, we are able to determine empirically

At least one formally stated theory of power already exists. Harsanyi (1962a), assuming rational utility-maximization and extending the Zeuthen–Nash bargaining theory, expresses Dahl's amount of power as a function of variables representing two actors' utilities for rewards and punishments. Thus, as Harsanyi emphasizes, these variables can be used to *explain* the observed effect of one actor on the other's behavior. Since, as I showed in chapter 6, Dahl's measure is a path regression coefficient, Harsanyi's theory serves as a prototype for the kind of power theory I advocate.[2]

Harsanyi's variables are not readily made operational. Even if they were, it is likely that precise comparisons of theoretical and empirical coefficients would be possible only for laboratory situations. But it does not seem excessively optimistic to hope that, using Harsanyi's or, preferably, more realistic theories,[3] it will soon be possible to make at least ordinal predictions of coefficients relating real-world preferences and outcomes.[4]

Another perspective on the distinction between descriptive and explanatory modes of analysis is provided by Stinchcombe (1968:55): "The measurement of concepts is generally by either the causes of the phenomena or by their effects. The improvement of measurements and the refinement of concepts thus constitute a particular case of improvement of causal knowledge." Descriptive power coefficients derived from outcome observations are effect measures; predictive indices

---

the conditions that make for influence—the characteristics of individuals and situations that permit us to predict that the influence of a particular individual will be large—then we can derive from these empirical relationships additional indirect measurements of influence."

2. Strictly speaking, this statement should be qualified, because Harsanyi's model includes preferences for the outcome, which means that it is a theory of a particular instance of power exercise (Harsanyi's "power in a point sense"), rather than a theory of power coefficients alone.

3. Harsanyi's theory is based on an extremely simplistic carrot-and-stick psychology.

4. After writing this passage, I learned that Rosen (1972) has tested a theory similar to Harsanyi's using data from international politics. Laboratory research supporting the Harsanyi model has been reported by Bonoma, Tedeschi, and Lindskold (1972).

deduced from a theory of power are cause measures. Both kinds can be found in power research, but existing cause measures are often based on crude theories.[5] As I argue next, cause measures generally indicate power potential, while effect measures usually assess exercised power. Despite confusion over this point in the literature, the two approaches are compatible. They view the same phenomenon—causation of outcomes by preferences—from two different perspectives.

Potential Power

The idea of theories of power helps in understanding potential power, which has been the subject of unnecessary controversy. Critics of Simon, Dahl, and other empiricists contend that their focus on effects strips power of its traditional denotation of a potentiality or capability. Some empiricists are only too happy to accept the charge. Polsby (1963:60) categorically rejects the notion of potential power:

> How can one tell, after all, whether or not an actor is powerful unless some sequence of events, competently observed, attests to his power? If these events take place, then the power of the actor is not "potential" but actual. If these events do not occur, then what grounds have we to suppose that the actor is powerful? There appear to be no scientific grounds for such a supposition.

Contrary to Polsby, there can be excellent grounds for attributing potential power—provided that one has an applicable, well-substantiated theory of power. Statements about power potentials are, or should be, equivalent to predictions about power coefficients. Any use of "power" or "influence" to indicate a potential or capacity must therefore be an empirical hypothesis, derived from an implicit or explicit theory of power, one that may be strongly or weakly supported by past experience. Heretofore, writers employing a

5. E.g., Kingsley Davis' gross income measure of national military power, cited by Stinchcombe (1968: 218–19).

concept of potential power have generally left their theories implicit and untested.

Attribution of potential power is not sufficient to predict an outcome nor even to predict that an actor will influence an outcome. Recall that our basic model for an outcome Y_j is composed of terms of the type $d_{ji}U_i$. To assign potential power to an actor i amounts to predicting a positive value for d_{ji}. But to predict the outcome one must also know his preference U_i. If i has no preference concerning Y_j, or if his preference is weak, his causal effect on Y_j will be nil or insignificant.[6] Thus statements about *potential* power require only a theory of power coefficients, while statements about *predicted* or *probable* power require both a theory of power and a theory of preferences (or at least knowledge about preferences).

The preceding interpretation of potential influence conforms to common usage among students of power, whose statements about potential power are frequently of the type, "He *could* influence Y if only he cared enough about it."[7] Dahl (1970) illustrates the idea of potential influence by contrasting two hypothetical brothers, one wealthy but caring only for elegant living and the ballet, the second poor but passionately interested in politics. Combine the power potential of the first with the preferences of the second, Dahl suggests, and a high level of actual influence will result—just as is implied by the multiplicative formula.

This is not to say that all existing notions of potential power are exactly like this. In general, though, the term seems to imply a probability that the power will become effective if some psychic (and therefore supposedly labile) factor changes—e.g., if the potential power wielder loses an inhibition against exercising power, or if she becomes aware of her latent strength.

6. Power as a potential thus conforms to the general pattern of "potential" concepts, as described by Stinchcombe (1968: 230–31). His view (derived from the work of Duncan, Cuzzort, and Duncan) seems to be that the effects of potential concepts must be described using multiplicative functions of two or more variables.
7. Cf. Bachrach and Baratz (1962) and Kornberg and Perry (1966).

The actor's preference is the factor of this type that fits most readily into our framework.

Potential power that requires for effectiveness only a sufficiently intense preference must be distinguished from what Wrong (1968:680) calls *possible* power. From Wrong's account, one can infer that an actor with possible power lacks one or more requisites of effective power other than, or in addition to the necessary preference; and the missing element or elements can only be supplied through a temporally extended process. For example:

> In the case of social groups or categories, the achievement of solidarity, common goals, social organization, and leadership is necessary to convert possible power into realized power ... ; a long process of social mobilization and indoctrination would have to take place before it could become a reality.

Attributions of possible power require or imply a *dynamic* theory of power coefficients, whereas statements about immediately utilizable potential power need only a static theory of power.[8] To say that an actor has possible power is to make a conditional prediction—*if* during time period $(t_1 - t_0)$, missing elements $e_1, e_2, \ldots e_n$ are supplied (organization, leadership, resources, skill, or whatever), then at t_1, the actor will be able to influence the outcome in question.[9] In contrast, statements about potential power also make conditional predictions, but these forecasts depend only upon the existence of preferences concerning the outcome.

Thus, ascending levels of theoretical complexity are implied by different types of power attribution. A simple model of the outcome suffices to estimate exercised power from known preferences and outcomes. To explain exercised power or to attribute potential power, a static theory of power coefficients

8. Wrong prefers to call the latter *latent* power.
9. Emerson (1962) and Dahl (1961: ch. 27) sketch interesting dynamic theories of power. March's (1966) resource depletion and conditioning models also fit in this category.

is needed, one that must include other variables. To predict exercised power in the near future, one must add hypotheses about preferences. To attribute possible power, one needs a dynamic model of power coefficients; and to make long-term predictions of exercised power (should one wish to be so rash), the dynamic theory of power must be supplemented by extended predictions about preferences.

Definitions and Hypotheses

As Dahl (1970:8) has observed, failure to distinguish between definitions and hypotheses is common in political analysis. Nowhere is the tendency more prevalent than in the study of power. An odd prestige attaches to the "concept" of power, so that writers prefer to present ideas as definitions even when they might be posed as empirical propositions.

Whatever the past reasons for this verbal preoccupation, future progress in understanding power will be facilitated if thinking about the subject is redirected from conceptual schemes to testable theories. The definition of power proposed in this book can promote such a reorientation.

Words, as Humpty Dumpty observed, can mean anything we choose them to mean. Why then bother to dispute definitions? I do so precisely because definitions are merely arbitrary, whereas hypotheses are potentially subject to agreement-producing tests. Therefore, the most useful definitions are those which direct efforts to empirical research. Defining power as causation of outcomes by preferences turns attention on the one hand to measures of exercised power, and on the other to factors which explain such relations.

This point of view places in coherent perspective a number of alternative definitions that identify power with capacities that help *explain* an actor's ability to realize preferences.[10] Examples, especially dominant in social psychology, include the power concepts of Cartwright (1959), Thibaut and Kelley

10. Pollard and Mitchell (1972) call them "process" definitions, as opposed to the "outcome" definitions of March, Dahl, and Simon.

(1959), and Karlsson (1962).[11] Presented as definitions, their superficially different ideas sow confusion. But if the meaning of power is kept constant as the causation of outcomes by preferences, then in principle we can test to determine how much, and under what conditions, each postulated ability contributes to the causation of preferred outcomes.[12]

ASSESSMENT

Our inquiry is nearly complete. Let us conclude by answering two key questions.

Is Confusion Necessary?

Power has been, and no doubt (despite this book!) will continue to be used with a great variety of meanings, some differing subtly, others radically. But major definitions, especially those expressed in formal symbols, are closely related, despite appearances to the contrary.

The five definitions Riker found to be "mutually exclusive" coexist amicably within our framework. Three—Dahl's M, the Shapley-Shubik index, and March's ranking criterion—are measures of power, actual or potential, over outcomes. March's and Dahl's are formally compatible with the measures I have proposed; the Shapley-Shubik index is at least weakly ordinally equivalent. Riker's remaining definitions—Cartwright's and Karlsson's—are best viewed as elements in the theory of power, where they might function as partial predictors of outcome measures.

Differences detected by Dahl (1968) similarly are not serious impediments. He divides approaches to power measurement into three types—game theoretic (Shapley-

---

11. Even Harsanyi (1962a, 1962b) is ambivalent about whether to construe his ideas as hypotheses or definitions. He refers to his theorems as a model or theory, but he also insists that the key factors in his formulas "are essential ingredients of the definition of power."

12. Indeed, the three concepts mentioned are closely related to elements in Harsanyi's more complex theory of power.

Shubik), Newtonian (his own, Simon, March), and economic (Harsanyi). The first two categories reach similar results by different routes. The third, is best treated as an explanatory and predictive theory, and as a measure only insofar as inductive research corroborates its deductive predictions.[13]

Conceptual disputes stemming from ideological controversy are also synthesized in this volume. From scholars generally identified with the pluralist view of American society, I have taken the basic conception of power as causation; the distinction between possession of resources and the actual exercise of power; insistence on rigor; and recognition that similarities in power distribution over different outcomes must be proven, not assumed. Inspired by more radical critics of American politics, I have sought to develop a concept broad enough to include power exercised without overt conflict and over outcomes that do not reach the agenda of decision makers; influence that occurs through anticipated reactions; and dominance imposed indirectly through agents and by control over attitudes, information, and access to resources.

Conceptual confusion seems much less a barrier to understanding, observing, and measuring power than is often thought.

How Useful Is "Power"?

An answer to this question should begin with descriptive power analysis. If we cannot show that preferences are significant causes of outcomes, it is hardly worthwhile to explain why some actors' preferences are more effective causes than others'. Moreover, describing power distributions is intrinsically at least as interesting as using the concept to predict or explain events.[14]

The concepts, measures, and methods proposed in this book enable one to specify with some precision conditions under

13. It should also be pointed out that Harsanyi's own work integrates Dahl's three approaches within a single theory.
14. A fact overlooked by March (1966), who appraised the "power of 'power'" only as a predictive concept.

which descriptive power analysis can be a profitable enterprise.

1. Relations between preferences and outcomes must be describable by block-recursive, identifiable models (chapters 4 and 5).

2. The data must show that preferences causally explain a significant portion of outcome variance (chapters 5 and 10).

3. Unless one wishes only to assess the cooperative power of a collectivity, preferences of significant actors must differ or be causally ordered (chapters 7 and 10).

4. An excessive time interval must not elapse between observations of preferences and outcomes (chapter 7).

5. Relative to the time unit of observation, preferences must be stable, in the sense that they do not interact strongly and quickly with each other, or with outcomes (chapter 9).

6. Influence coefficients must be reasonably constant within the time interval and outcome category studied (chapter 8).

These conditions no doubt obtain for some outcome variables and not for others. Decisions about whether or not they are satisfied should not be based on casual impressions, but instead should result from careful consideration of evidence.[15] When these requirements are met, and provided other difficulties described in preceding chapters can be overcome, the methods presented in this book make it possible to measure power on a scale not previously contemplated, and with a theoretical sophistication lacking in earlier research.

---

15. This is especially so because of biases affecting sensitivity to power. Barber (1966: 47) reports that local officials he studied perceived power only in their relations with external units: within their own groups, they saw only problems of logical persuasion and deliberation. And Kahn (1964: 3) plausibly argues that intensity of motivation to seek power depends on the degree of conflict existing between one's wishes and the behavior of others. These two conclusions suggest that awareness of power in a system varies inversely with integration into the system and sympathy for prevailing outcomes. These hypotheses help explain why some social scientists downplay the importance of power, while others emphasize it.

As for the explanatory and predictive usefulness of power, it is apparent that in all probability we are, as March (1966) says, "not within shouting distance" of an adequately complex theory. Indeed, no one theory is likely to suffice. There are simply too many processes by which preferences can cause outcomes. Even the decision-making approach, probably the broadest existing integrative framework, fails to encompass physical force and some collective choice systems (Pollard and Mitchell, 1972).[16] Nevertheless, power analysts have recently taken significant steps toward building explanatory theory;[17] and more progress can be expected, especially if others are persuaded that we now need less conceptualizing and more true theorizing and theory testing.

16. The probable lack of a single predictive theory of power emphasizes the need for inductive power measurement, which can show the resultant influence when two or more partial theories yield conflicting predictions.
17. If I were attempting to construct an explanatory theory of power, I would begin by consulting the following works: Harsanyi (1962a, 1962b), Alker (1973), Pollard and Mitchell (1972), Dahl (1960, 1961, 1970), Emerson (1962), Gamson (1968), Olson (1965), Coleman (1966, 1970), Stinchcombe (1968), March (1966), Cartwright (1959), French and Raven (1959), Thibaut and Kelley (1959), Blau (1964), Dahlstrom (1966), Schelling (1966), Baldwin (1971a, 1971b, 1971c), and the reviews by Collins and Guetzkow (1964), Collins and Raven (1969), Cartwright (1965), and Schopler (1965).

REFERENCES

Items marked with one asterisk are also reprinted in the anthology *Political Power*, edited by Bell, Edwards, and Wagner (1969). Articles marked with a double asterisk are also included in the Blalock (1971) collection, *Causal Models in the Social Sciences*.

Abelson, Robert P. 1964. "Mathematical Models of the Distribution of Attitudes under Controversy." In *Contributions to Mathematical Psychology*, edited by Norman Frederiksen and Harold Gulliksen. New York: Holt, Rinehart, and Winston.

Ackoff, Russell. 1953. *The Design of Social Research*. Chicago: University of Chicago Press.

Alker, Hayward R., Jr. 1965. *Mathematics and Politics*. New York: Macmillan.

———. 1966. "Causal Inference and Political Analysis." In *Mathematical Applications in Political Science II*, edited by Joseph L. Bernd. Dallas: Southern Methodist University Press.

———. 1969. "Statistics and Politics: The Need for Causal Data Analysis." In *Politics and the Social Sciences*, edited by Seymour Martin Lipset. New York: Oxford.

———. 1973. "On Political Capabilities in a Schedule Sense: Measuring Power, Integration and Development." In *Mathematical Approaches to Politics*, edited by Hayward R. Alker, Jr., Karl W. Deutsch, and Antoine H. Stoetzel. San Francisco: Jossey-Bass.

Allingham, M. G. 1973. "Power and Value." Philadelphia: University of Pennsylvania, Fels Discussion Paper no. 43.

Althauser, Robert P. 1971. "Multicollinearity and Nonadditive Regression Models." In *Causal Models in the Social Sciences*, edited by Hubert M. Blalock. Chicago: Aldine-Atherton.**

Ando, Albert; Fisher, Franklin M.; and Simon, Herbert A. 1963. *Essays on the Structure of Social Science Models*. Cambridge, Mass.: MIT Press.

Arrow, Kenneth. 1963. *Social Choice and Individual Values*, 2nd edition. New York: Wiley.

Axelrod, Robert. 1970. *Conflict of Interest*. Chicago: Markham.

Bachrach, Peter, and Baratz, Morton. 1962. "Two Faces of Power." *American Political Science Review* 56: 947–52.*

———. 1963. "Decisions and Nondecisions: An Analytical Frame-work." *American Political Science Review* 57: 632-42.*

Balbus, Isaac. 1971. "The Concept of Interest in Pluralist and Marxian Analysis." *Politics and Society 1*: 151–78.

Baldwin, David A. 1971a. "The Costs of Power." *Journal of Conflict Resolution 15*: 145–55.

———. 1971b. "Money and Power." *Journal of Politics 33*: 578–614.

———. 1971c. "The Power of Positive Sanctions." *World Politics 24*: 19–38.

Banfield, Edward. 1961. *Political Influence*. New York: The Free Press.*

Banzhaf, John F. 1965. "Weighted Majority Voting Doesn't Work: A Mathematical Analysis." *Rutgers Law Review 19*: 317–43.

———. 1966. "Multi-member Electoral Districts: Do They Violate the 'One Man, One Vote' Principle?" *Yale Law Journal 75*: 1309–38.

———. 1968. "One Man, 3.312 Votes: A Mathematical Analysis of the Electoral College." *Villanova Law Review 13*: 304–32.

Barber, J. David. 1966. *Power in Committees*. Chicago: Rand McNally.

Barnet, Richard J. 1971. "The National Security Managers and the National Interest." *Politics and Society 1*: 257–68.

Bateson, Gregory; Jackson, Don D.; Haley, Jay; and Weakland, John. 1956. "Toward a Theory of Schizophrenia." *Behavioral Science 1*: 251–64.

Bell, Roderick. 1969. "Political Power: The Problem of Measurement." In *Political Power*, edited by Roderick Bell et al. New York: The Free Press.*

Bell, Roderick; Edwards, David V.; and Wagner, R. Harrison. 1969. *Political Power: A Reader in Theory and Research*. New York: The Free Press.

Bierstedt, Robert. 1950. "An Analysis of Social Power." *American Sociological Review 15*: 730–38.

Blalock, Hubert M. 1960. *Social Statistics*. New York: McGraw-Hill.

———. 1961. *Causal Inferences in Nonexperimental Research*. Chapel Hill: University of North Carolina Press.

———. 1967a. "Causal Inferences, Closed Populations, and Measures of Association." *American Political Science Review 61*: 130–36.

———. 1967b. "Path Coefficients vs. Regression Coefficients." *American Journal of Sociology 72*: 675–76.

———. 1968a. "The Measurement Problem." In *Methodology in Social Research*, edited by Hubert M. and Ann B. Blalock. New York: McGraw-Hill.

———. 1968b. "Theory Building and Causal Inferences." In *Methodology in Social Research*, edited by Hubert M. and Ann B. Blalock. New York: McGraw-Hill.

————. 1969. *Theory Construction*. Englewood Cliffs, N.J.: Prentice-Hall.

————. 1970. "Estimating Measurement Error Using Multiple Indicators and Several Points in Time." *American Sociological Review 35*: 101–11.

Blalock, Hubert M., ed. 1971. *Causal Models in the Social Sciences*. Chicago: Aldine-Atherton.

Blau, Peter. 1964. *Exchange and Power in Social Life*. New York: Wiley.*

Blau, Peter, and Duncan, Otis Dudley. 1967. *The American Occupational Structure*. New York: Wiley.

Bonoma, Thomas V.; Tedeschi, James T.; and Lindskold, Svenn. 1972, "A Note Regarding an Expected Value Model of Social Power." *Behavioral Science 17*: 221–28.

Borgatta, Edgar F., and Bohrnstedt, George W. 1970. *Sociological Methodology 1970*. San Francisco: Jossey-Bass.

Boudon, Raymond. 1965. "A Method of Linear Causal Analysis." *American Sociological Review 30*: 365–74.

————. 1967. *L'Analyse Mathématique des Faits Sociaux*. Paris: Librairie Plon.

————. 1968. "A New Look at Correlation Analysis." In *Methodology in Social Research*, edited by Hubert M. and Ann B. Blalock. New York: McGraw-Hill.

Boyle, Richard P. 1970. "Path Analysis and Ordinal Data." *American Journal of Sociology 75*: 461–80.**

————. 1971. "Rejoinder to Werts and Linn, Lyons and Carter." *American Journal of Sociology 76*: 1132–34.

Brams, Steven J. 1968. "Measuring the Concentration of Power in Political Systems." *American Political Science Review 62*: 461–75.*

Braybrooke, David. 1968. *Three Tests for Democracy*. New York: Random House.

Brodbeck, May. 1968. "Methodological Individualisms: Definition and Reduction." In *Readings in the Philosophy of the Social Sciences*, edited by May Brodbeck. New York: Macmillan.

Buckley, Walter B. 1967. *Sociology and Modern Systems Theory*. Englewood Cliffs, N.J.: Prentice-Hall.

Buckley, Walter B., ed. 1968. *Modern Systems Research for the Behavioral Scientist*. Chicago: Aldine.

Cartwright, Dorwin, ed. 1959. *Studies in Social Power*. Ann Arbor: University of Michigan Press.

————. 1965. "Influence, Leadership, Control." In *Handbook of Organizations*, edited by James G. March. Chicago: Rand McNally.*

Cervin, Vladimir. 1957. "Relationship of Ascendant-Submissive Behavior in Dyadic Groups of Human Subjects to Their Emotional

Responsiveness." *Journal of Abnormal and Social Psychology 54*: 241–49.

Cervin, Vladimir, and Henderson, G. P. 1961. "Statistical Theory of Persuasion." *Psychological Review 68*: 157–66.

Champlin, John. 1971. "On the Study of Power." *Politics and Society 1*: 91–111.

Churchman, C. West, and Ackoff, Russell. 1950. "Purposive Behavior and Cybernetics." *Social Forces 29*: 32–39.

Cnudde, Charles F., and McCrone, Donald J. 1966. "The Linkage between Constituency Attitudes and Congressional Voting Behavior: A Causal Model." *American Political Science Review 60*: 66–72.*

Coleman, James S. 1966. "Foundations for a Theory of Collective Decisions." *American Journal of Sociology 71*: 615–27.

————. 1970. "Political Money." *American Political Science Review 64*: 1074–87.

Collins, Barry E., and Guetzkow, Harold. 1964. *A Social Psychology of Group Processes for Decision-Making*. New York: Wiley.

Collins, Barry E., and Raven, Bertram H. 1969. "Group Structure, Attraction, Coalitions, Communication, and Power." In *The Handbook of Social Psychology*, edited by Gardner Lindzey and Eliot Aronson, 2nd edition, volume 4. Reading, Mass.: Addison-Wesley.

Commoner, Barry. 1971. *The Closing Circle*. New York: Bantam.

Dahl, Robert A. 1957. "The Concept of Power." *Behavioral Science 2*: 201–15.*

————. 1958. "A Critique of the Ruling Elite Model." *American Political Science Review 58*: 463–69.*

————. 1960. "The Analysis of Influence in Local Communities." In *Social Science and Community Action*, edited by Charles R. Adrian. East Lansing, Mich.: Michigan State University Press.

————. 1961. *Who Governs?* New Haven: Yale University Press.

————. 1965. "Cause and Effect in the Study of Politics." In *Cause and Effect*, edited by Daniel Lerner. New York: The Free Press.

————. 1968. "Power." *International Encyclopedia of the Social Sciences*. New York: The Free Press.

————. 1970. *Modern Political Analysis*, 2nd edition, Englewood Cliffs, N.J.: Prentice-Hall.

Dahlstrom, Edmund. 1966. "Exchange, Influence, and Power." *Acta Sociologica 9*: 237–84.

Davidson, D.; Suppes, P.; and Siegel, S. 1957. *Decision-Making: An Experimental Approach*. Stanford: Stanford University Press.

Davis, Otto A.; Dempster, M. A. H.; and Wildavsky, Aaron. 1966. "A Theory of the Budgetary Process." *American Political Science Review 60*: 529–47.

Deutsch, Karl W. 1966. "Some Quantitative Constraints on Value Allocation in Society and Politics." *Behavioral Science 11*: 245–52.

———. 1970. *Politics and Government*. Boston: Houghton Mifflin.

Domhoff, G. William. 1967. *Who Rules America?* Englewood Cliffs, N.J.: Prentice-Hall.

Duncan, Otis Dudley. 1966. "Path Analysis: Sociological Examples." *American Journal of Sociology 72*: 1–16.**

———. 1969. "Contingencies in Constructing Causal Models." In *Sociological Methodology 1969*, edited by Edgar Borgatta and George Bohrnstedt. San Francisco: Jossey-Bass.

———. 1970. "Partials, Partitions, and Paths." In *Sociological Methodology, 1970*, edited by Edgar F. Borgatta and George W. Bohrnstedt. San Francisco: Jossey-Bass.

Duncan, Otis Dudley; Haller, Archibald; and Portes, Alejandro. 1968. "Peer Influences on Aspirations: A Reinterpretation." *American Journal of Sociology 74*: 119–37.**

Easton, David. 1953. *The Political System*. New York: Knopf.

Edwards, Elwyn. 1964. *Information Transmission*. London: Chapman and Hall.

Emerson, Richard E. 1962. "Power-dependence Relations." *American Sociological Review 27*: 31–41.

Etzioni, Amitai. 1968. *The Active Society*. New York: The Free Press.

Farquharson, Robin. 1969. *Theory of Voting*. New Haven: Yale University Press.

Festinger, Leon, and Carlsmith, J. M. 1959. "Cognitive Consequences of Forced Compliance." *Journal of Abnormal and Social Psychology 58*: 203–10.

Feuer, Lewis. 1965. "Causality in the Social Sciences." In *Cause and Effect*, edited by Daniel Lerner. New York: The Free Press.

Fisher, Franklin M. 1966. *The Identification Problem in Econometrics*. New York: McGraw-Hill.

Forbes, Hugh Donald, and Tufte, Edward R. 1968a. "A Note of Caution in Causal Modeling." *American Political Science Review 62*: 1258–64.

———. 1968b. "Communication." *American Political Science Review 62*: 1269–70.

French, John R. P., Jr. 1956. "A Formal Theory of Social Power." *Psychological Review 63*: 181–94.

French, John R. P., Jr., and Raven, Bertram H. 1959. "The Bases of Social Power." In *Studies in Social Power*, edited by Dorwin Cartwright. Ann Arbor: University of Michigan Press.

Frey, Frederick. 1971. "Nondecisions and the Study of Local Politics: Comment." *American Political Science Review 65*: 1081–1101.

Friedrich, Carl J. 1963. *Man and His Government*. New York: McGraw-Hill.

Fujihira, Donald T. 1974. "The Shapley–Shubik Power Index: Some Different Interpretations." Philadelphia: University of Pennsylvania, unpublished paper.

Gamson, William A. 1968. *Power and Discontent*. Homewood, Ill.: Dorsey.

Gasking, Douglas. 1955. "Causation and Recipes." *Mind 64*: 479–88.

Gitlin, Todd. 1965. "Local Pluralism as Theory and Ideology." *Studies on the Left 5*: 21–45.

Goldberger, Arthur S. 1964. *Econometric Theory*. New York: Wiley.
———. 1970. "On Boudon's Method of Linear Causal Analysis." *American Sociological Review 35*: 97–101.

Goldberger, Arthur S., and Duncan, Otis Dudley, editors. 1973. *Structural Equation Models in the Social Sciences*. New York: Seminar Press.

Goldhamer, Herbert, and Shils, Edward. 1939. "Types of Power and Status." *American Journal of Sociology 45*: 171–82.

Gordon, R. A. 1968. "Issues in Multiple Regression." *American Journal of Sociology 73*: 592–616.

Green, Philip. 1968. "A Singular Pluralism." *World Politics 20*: 301–26.

Greene, Felix. 1961. *Awakened China*. Garden City, N.Y.: Doubleday.

Haitovsky, Yoel. 1969. "A Note on the Maximization of $\bar{R}^2$." *The American Statistician 23*: 20–21.

Harary, Frank. 1959. "A Criterion for Unanimity in French's Theory of Social Power." In *Studies in Social Power*, edited by Dorwin Cartwright. Ann Arbor: University of Michigan Press.

Hardin, Russell. 1971. "Collective Action as an Agreeable n-Prisoners' Dilemma." *Behavioral Science 16*: 472–81.

Harsanyi, John G. 1962a. "Measurement of Social Power, Opportunity Costs, and the Theory of Two-Person Bargaining Games." *Behavioral Science 7*: 67–80.*
———. 1962b. "Measurement of Social Power in N-Person Reciprocal Power Situations." *Behavioral Science 7*: 81–92.*

Hawkes, Roland K. 1970. "The Multivariate Analysis of Ordinal Measures." *American Journal of Sociology 76*: 908–26.

Hays, William L. 1963. *Statistics for Psychologists*. New York: Holt, Rinehart, and Winston.

Heider, Fritz. 1958. *The Psychology of Interpersonal Relations*. New York: Wiley.

Heise, David R. 1969. "Problems in Path Analysis and Causal Inference." In *Sociological Methodology 1969*, edited by Edgar R. Borgatta and George Bohrnstedt. San Francisco: Jossey-Bass.

Hempel, Carl G. 1952. "Fundamentals of Concept Formation in Empirical Science." *International Encyclopedia of Unified Science*, Vol. 2. Chicago: University of Chicago Press.

Henderson, James M., and Quandt, Richard E. 1958. *Microeconomic Theory*. New York: McGraw-Hill.

Hickson, David J. 1970. Book review. *Administrative Science Quarterly* *15*: 120–21.

Hilgard, Ernest R. and Bower, Gordon H. 1966. *Theories of Learning*, 3rd edition. New York: Appleton-Century Crofts.

Hobbes, Thomas. 1651. *Leviathan*. Collier Books Edition, 1962. New York: Crowell-Collier.

Hume, David. 1777. *An Enquiry concerning Human Understanding*. Religion of Science Library Edition. LaSalle, Ill.: Open Court.

Hunter, Floyd. 1953. *Community Power Structure*. Chapel Hill: University of North Carolina Press.

Huntington, Samuel. 1968. *Political Order in Changing Societies*. New Haven: Yale University Press.

Irwin, Francis W. 1958. "An Analysis of the Concepts of Discrimination and Preference." *American Journal of Psychology 71*: 152–63.

———. 1971. *Intentional Behavior and Motivation: A Cognitive Theory*. Philadelphia: Lippincott.

Jackson, John E. 1971. "Statistical Models of Senate Roll Call Voting." *American Political Science Review 65*: 451–70.

Johnston, J. 1963. *Econometric Methods*. New York: McGraw-Hill.

Juster, Richard. 1970. "Causal Relations and Structural Models." *Proceedings, Social Statistics Section, American Statistical Association*, 81–91.

Kadushin, Charles. 1968. "Power, Influence and Social Circles: A New Methodology for Studying Opinion Makers." *American Sociological Review 33*: 685–99.

Kahn, Robert L. 1964. "Introduction." In *Power and Conflict in Organizations*, edited by R. L. Kahn and Elise Boulding. New York: Basic Books.

Kaplan, Abraham. 1964. *The Conduct of Inquiry*. San Francisco: Chandler.

Karlsson, Georg. 1962. "Some Aspects of Power in Small Groups." In *Mathematical Methods in Small Group Processes*, edited by Joan H. Criswell, Herbert Salomon, and Patrick Suppes. Stanford: Stanford University Press.

Kornberg, Allen, and Perry, Simon D. 1966. "Conceptual Models of Power and Their Applicability to Empirical Research in Politics." *Political Science 18*: 52–70.

Labovitz, Sanford. 1970. "The Assignment of Numbers to Rank Order Categories." *American Sociological Review 35*: 515–24.

Lammers, C. J. 1967. "Power and Participation in Decision-Making in Formal Organizations." *American Journal of Sociology 73*: 201–16.

Land, Kenneth C. 1969. "Principles of Path Analysis." In *Sociological Methodology, 1969*, edited by Edgar Borgatta and George F. Bohrnstedt. San Francisco: Jossey-Bass.

Lasswell, Harold, and Kaplan, Abraham. 1950. *Power and Society*. New Haven: Yale University Press.

Latham, Earl. 1952. "The Group Basis of Politics: Notes for a Theory." *American Political Science Review 46*: 376–97.

Lehman, Edward W. 1969. "Toward a Macrosociology of Power." *American Sociological Review 34*: 453–65.

Lerner, Daniel, ed. 1965. *Cause and Effect*. New York: The Free Press.

Li, Ching Chun. 1955. *Population Genetics*. Chicago: University of Chicago Press.

Luce, R. Duncan, and Raiffa, Howard. 1957. *Games and Decisions*. New York: Wiley.

Luce, R. Duncan, and Suppes, Patrick. 1965. "Preference, Utility, and Subjective Probability." In *Handbook of Mathematical Psychology*, Vol. 3. New York: Wiley.

Lyons, Morgan. 1971. "Techniques for Using Ordinal Measures in Regression and Path Analysis." In *Sociological Methodology, 1971*, edited by Herbert L. Costner. San Francisco: Jossey-Bass.

Lyons, Morgan, and Carter, T. Michael. 1971. "Further Comments on Boyle's 'Path Analysis and Ordinal Data.'" *American Journal of Sociology 76*: 1112–32.

McFarland, Andrew S. 1969. *Power and Leadership in Pluralist Systems*. Stanford: Stanford University Press.

Mao Tse-tung. 1943. "Some Questions concerning Methods of Leadership," In *Selected Readings from the Works of Mao Tse-tung*. Peking: Foreign Languages Press, 1967.

March, James G. 1955. "An Introduction to the Theory and Measurement of Influence." *American Political Science Review 49*: 431–51.*

———. 1957. "Measurement Concepts in the Theory of Influence." *Journal of Politics 19*: 202–26.*

———. 1966. "The Power of Power." In *Varieties of Political Theory*, edited by David Easton. Englewood Cliffs, N.J.: Prentice-Hall.

Marcuse, Herbert. 1964. *One-Dimensional Man*. Boston: Beacon Press.

Mayhew, Bruce H., Jr.; Gray, Louis N.; and Richardson, James T. 1969. "Behavioral Measurement of Operating Power Structures." *Sociometry 32*: 474–89.

Merelman, Richard M. 1968. "On the Neo-elitist Critique of Community Power." *American Political Science Review 62*: 451–60.

Miller, Warren E., and Stokes, Donald E. 1963. "Constituency Influence in Congress." *American Political Science Review 57*: 45–56.

Mills, C. Wright. 1956. *The Power Elite*. New York: Oxford University Press.

Morgenthau, Hans J. 1958. "Power as a Political Concept." In *Approaches to the Study of Politics*, edited by Roland Young. Evanston, Ill.: Northwestern University Press.

Myrdal, Jan. 1965. *Report from a Chinese Village*. New York: New American Library.

Nagel, Ernest. 1965. "Types of Causal Explanation in Science." In *Cause and Effect*, edited by Daniel Lerner. New York: The Free Press.

Nagel, Jack H. 1968. "Some Questions about the Concept of Power." *Behavioral Science 13*: 129–37.

———. 1972. *The Descriptive Analysis of Power*. New Haven: Yale University, Ph.D. dissertation.

———. 1974. "Inequality and Discontent: A Nonlinear Hypothesis." *World Politics 27*: 453–72.

Nardin, Terry. 1973. "Conflicting Conceptions of Political Violence." In *Political Science Annual*, volume 4, edited by Cornelius P. Cotter. Indianapolis: Bobbs-Merrill.

Neustadt, Richard E. 1960. *Presidential Power*. New York: Wiley.

Olson, Mancur, Jr. 1965. *The Logic of Collective Action*. Cambridge, Mass.: Harvard University Press.

Oppenheim, Felix E. 1958. "An Analysis of Political Control: Actual and Potential." *Journal of Politics 20*: 515–34.

———. 1961. *Dimensions of Freedom*. New York: St. Martin's Press.

Overseth, Oliver E. 1969. "Experiments in Time Reversal." *Scientific American 221*: 88–101.

Parsons, Talcott. 1957. "The Distribution of Power in American Society." *World Politics 10*: 123–43.

———. 1963a. "On the Concept of Influence." *Public Opinion Quarterly 27*: 37–62.

———. 1963b. "On the Concept of Political Power." *Proceedings of the American Philosophical Society 107*: 232–62.*

Payne, James L. 1968. "The Oligarchy Muddle." *World Politics 20*: 439–53.

Pettigrew, Andrew. 1972. "Information Control as a Power Resource." *Sociology 6*: 187–204.

Pilisuk, Marc, and Hayden, Thomas. 1965. "Is There a Military-Industrial Complex Which Prevents Peace?" *Journal of Social Issues 21*: 67–117.

Pollard, William E., and Mitchell, Terence R. 1972. "Decision Theory Analysis of Social Power." *Psychological Bulletin 78*: 433–46.

Polsby, Nelson. 1963. *Community Power and Political Theory*. New Haven: Yale University Press.

Przeworski, Adam, and Soares, Glaucio. 1971. "Theories in Search of a Curve: A Contextual Interpretation of Left Vote." *American Political Science Review 60*: 640–54.

Pye, Lucien. 1967. "The Formation of New States." In *Contemporary Political Science*, edited by Ithiel de Sola Pool. New York: McGraw-Hill.

Rapoport, Anatol. 1960. *Strategy and Conscience*. New York: Harper and Row.

Rescher, Nicholas. 1967. "Semantic Foundations for the Logic of Preference." In *The Logic of Decision and Action*, edited by Nicholas Rescher. Pittsburgh: University of Pittsburgh Press.

Riker, William. 1964. "Some Ambiguities in the Notion of Power." *American Political Science Review 58*: 341–49.*

Riker, William, and Shapley, Lloyd. 1968. "Weighted Voting: A Mathematical Analysis for Instrumental Judgments." In *Nomos X: Representation*, edited by J. Roland Pennock and John W. Chapman. New York: Atherton.

Rosen, Steven. 1972. "War Power and the Willingness to Suffer." In *Peace, War, and Numbers*, edited by Bruce Russett. Beverly Hills, Cal.: Sage.

Rosenblueth, Arturo, and Wiener, Norbert. 1950. "Purposeful and Non-purposeful Behavior." *Philosophy of Science 17*: 318–26.

Russett, Bruce. 1968. "Probabilism and the Number of Units Affected; Measuring Influence Concentration." *American Political Science Review 62*: 476–80.

Samuelson, Paul A. 1965. "Some Notions of Causality and Teleology in Economics." In *Cause and Effect*, edited by Daniel Lerner. New York: The Free Press.

Sartori, Giovanni. 1962. *Democratic Theory*. New York: Praeger.

Schelling, Thomas C. 1966. *Arms and Influence*. New Haven: Yale University Press.

Schlipp, Paul Arthur. 1963. *The Philosophy of Rudolf Carnap*. LaSalle, Ill.: Open Court.

Schopler, John. 1965. "Social Power." In *Advances in Experimental Social Psychology*, Vol. 2, edited by Leonard Berkowitz. New York: Academic Press.

Shannon, Claude E., and Weaver, Warren. 1949. *The Mathematical Theory of Communication*. Urbana: University of Illinois Press.

Shapley, Lloyd. 1953. "A Value for *n*-Person Games." In *Contributions to the Theory of Games II*, edited by H. W. Kuhn and A. W. Tucker. Princeton: Princeton University Press.

Shapley, Lloyd, and Shubik, Martin. 1954. "A Method for Evaluating the Distribution of Power in a Committee System." *American Political Science Review 48*: 787–92.*

Simon, Herbert A. 1953. "Notes on the Observation and Measurement of Political Power." *Journal of Politics 15*: 500–16.*

———. 1957. *Models of Man*. New York: Wiley.

———. 1968. "Causation." *International Encyclopedia of the Social Sciences*. New York: Macmillan.

Simon, Herbert A., and Rescher, Nicholas. 1966. "Cause and Counterfactual." *Philosophy of Science 33*: 324–40.

Singer, J. David. 1963. "Inter-nation Influence." *American Political Science Review 57*: 420–30.

Skinner, B. F. 1953. *Science and Human Behavior*. New York: Macmillan.

Snow, Edgar. 1962. *The Other Side of the River*. New York: Random House.

Stinchcombe, Arthur. 1968. *Constructing Social Theories*. New York: Harcourt, Brace, and World.

Stokes, Donald E. 1971. "Compound Paths in Political Analysis." In *Mathematical Applications in Political Science V*, edited by James F. Herndon and Joseph L. Bernd. Charlottesville, Va.: The University Press of Virginia.

Strotz, Robert H., and Wold, H. O. A. 1960. "Recursive versus Nonrecursive Systems: An Attempt at Synthesis." *Econometrica 28*: 417–27.**

Suppes, Patrick. 1957. *Introduction to Logic*. New York: Van Nostrand.

Talbot, Allan R. 1967. *The Mayor's Game*. New York: Harper and Row.

Tannenbaum, A. S. 1961. "Control and Effectiveness in a Voluntary Organization." *American Journal of Sociology 67*: 33–46.

———. 1962. "An Event-Structure Approach to Social Power and to the Problem of Power Comparability." *Behavioral Science 7*: 315–31.

Tannenbaum, A. S., and Georgopolous, B. S. 1957. "The Distribution of Control in Formal Organizations." *Social Forces 36*: 44–50.

Tannenbaum, A. S., and Kahn, R. L. 1957. "Organizational Control Structure." *Human Relations 10*: 127–40.

Taylor, Michael. 1968. "Towards a Mathematical Theory of Influence and Attitude Change." *Human Relations 21*: 121–39.

Theil, Henri. 1970. "On the Estimation of Relationships Using Qualitative Variables." *American Journal of Sociology 76*: 103–54.

Thibaut, John W., and Kelley, Harold H. 1959. *The Social Psychology of Groups*. New York: Wiley.

Timasheff, N. S. 1959. "Order, Causality, and Conjuncture." In *Symposium on Sociological Theory*, edited by Llewellyn Gross. White Plains, N.Y.: Row, Peterson, and Co.

Tufte, Edward R. 1969. "Improving Data Analysis in Political Science." *World Politics 21*: 641–54.

Tukey, John W. 1954. "Causation, Regression, and Path Analysis." In *Statistics and Mathematics in Biology*, edited by Oscar Kempthorne et al. Ames: Iowa State University Press.

Turner, Malcolm E., and Stevens, Charles D. 1959. "The Regression Analysis of Causal Paths." *Biometrics 15*: 236–58.**

Upshaw, Harry S. 1968. "Attitude Measurement." In *Methodology in Social Research*, edited by Hubert M. and Ann B. Blalock. New York: McGraw-Hill.

Van Doorn, J. A. A. 1963. "Sociology and the Problem of Power." *Sociologica Neerlandica 1*: 3–51.

Wagner, R. Harrison. 1969. "The Concept of Power and the Study of Politics." In *Political Power*, edited by R. Bell et al. New York: The Free Press.*

Weber, Max. 1947. *The Theory of Social and Economic Organization*, edited by Talcott Parsons. New York: The Free Press.

Werts, Charles E., and Linn, Robert L. 1971. "Comments on Boyle's 'Path Analysis and Ordinal Data.'" *American Journal of Sociology 76*: 1109–12.

———. 1972. "Erratum to the Werts–Linn Comments on Boyle's 'Path Analysis and Ordinal Data.'" *American Journal of Sociology 78*: 689–95.

Wheeler, Harvey. 1968. "Making the World One." *The Center Magazine 1*: 34–39.

Whisler, Thomas L. 1964. "Measuring Centralization of Control in Business Organizations." In *New Perspectives in Organization Research*, edited by W. W. Cooper et al. New York: Wiley.

Wilson, Thomas P. 1971. "Critique of Ordinal Variables." *Social Forces 49*: 432–44.**

Wright, Sewall. 1921. "Correlation and Causation." *Journal of Agricultural Research 20*: 557–85.

———. 1954. "The Interpretation of Multivariate Systems." In *Statistics and Mathematics in Biology*, edited by Oscar Kempthorne et al. Ames: Iowa State College Press.

———. 1960. "Path Coefficients and Path Regressions: Alternative or Complementary Concepts?" *Biometrics 16*: 189–202.**

———. 1960b. "The Treatment of Reciprocal Interaction, with or without Lag, in Path Analysis." *Biometrics 16*: 423–45.

———. 1968. *Evolution and the Genetics of Populations*. Chicago: University of Chicago Press.

Wrong, Dennis H. 1968. "Some Problems in Defining Social Power." *American Journal of Sociology 73*: 673–81.

INDEX

Ackoff, Russell, 23, 31
Actors: defined, 29; selection of, 118–20; power not a relation between, 143–44
Aggregative concept of power, 161n
Alker, Hayward R., Jr., 142
Allingham, Michael G., 98
Amount of power. *See* Dahl, Robert A.
Anticipated reactions, rule of: defined, 16; examples of, 16; neglected by behaviorists, 16–20; and reward and punishment, 23; and preferences, 24, 26–29, 31–34, 109; conditions favoring, 26n; paradoxes of, 31–33, 143–44; in definition of power, 34; voter influence through, 105; in shared power, 144–45; and overt conflict, 154; mentioned, 22, 49, 50, 101, 120, 146, 177
Aristotle, 3
Arms races, 142
Assets, power. *See* Resources
Attenuation of influence, 106–7
Authority, 8, 35
Autonomous power, measure of, 102–3
Autonomy, 29n, 168
Axelrod, Robert, 154

Bachrach, Peter, 87, 105, 116
Banfield, Edward C., 143
Banzhaf, John F., 98–99
Baratz, Morton, 87, 105, 116
Barbieri, Arthur T., 143
Bargaining, 142, 156
Barnet, Richard J., 104
Behavior: as effect variable, 12–14; as causal variable, 14–20;

temporal sequence of, 49; in reciprocal power relations, 143–46; included in "outcomes," 167
Bell, Roderick, 169
Benefit, 157–58, 165n
Beta weights, 65
Blalock, Hubert M., 51, 54
Blau, Peter, 141
Block-recursive systems: and causal ordering, 37n, 60; defined, 59; power hypotheses as, 60, 178; with endogenous preferences, 147–51
Boudon, Raymond, 55, 72, 95, 148
Bower, Gordon H., 19
Boyle, Richard P., 73

Candidate selection, 129–40
Capitalists, 107, 124
Carnap, Rudolf, 25
Cartwright, Dorwin, 4, 15, 175, 176
Case studies, 119
Causal inference: statistical, 51–53; in recursive models, 63; in path analysis, 74–79; about direction of causation, 77–78; in power research, 90; inconclusiveness of, 125; examples of, 128–35; mentioned, 10, 31n, 33, 35, 54. *See also* Overidentification; Simon–Blalock method; Test equations; Theory trimming
Causal laws: indicated by path regressions, 84; distinguished from causes, 87n
Causal ordering: defined, 37–39; extra-mathematical basis, 45–46; justifications for, 46–52; relation to identifiability, 57n; and exclusion of coefficients, 63;